The Grand Gesture

Deborah McAndrew studied Drama at Manchester University, before embarking on an acting career, which includes extensive work in radio and television, and in repertory and touring theatre. Her play writing credits include *Ugly, Duck* (ClayBody Theatre, 2013); *Beyond the Veil* (Mikron Theatre, 2013); *Losing The Plot* (Mikron Theatre, 2012); *David Copperfield* (Octagon Theatre, Bolton, 2010); *King Macbeth* (Reveal Theatre Co, 2010); *Oliver Twist* (Octagon Theatre, Bolton, 2009); *Flamingoland* (New Vic Theatre, 2008); and for Northern Broadsides, *A Government Inspector* (2012); *Accidental Death of an Anarchist* (2008); *Vacuum* (2006); *The Bells* (2004). Current commissions include *An August Bank Holiday Lark* (Northern Broadsides, touring 2014); *Till The Cows Come Home* (Mikron Theatre, touring 2014). Short films include *Sponge* (produced by Community Film Unit, 2013); *The Lantern* (BIGred Studio, 2011). Deborah is currently a guest lecturer at Staffordshire University Department of Drama, Performance and Theatre Arts, where she teaches Play Writing, Documentary Theatre and Acting.

T0276959

Deborah McAndrew

The Grand Gesture

Freely adapted from The Suicide
by Nikolai Erdman

B L O O M S B U R Y
LONDON • NEW DELHI • NEW YORK • SYDNEY

Bloomsbury Methuen Drama
An imprint of Bloomsbury Publishing Plc

50 Bedford Square	1385 Broadway
London	New York
WC1B 3DP	NY 10018
UK	USA

www.bloomsbury.com

Bloomsbury is a registered trade mark of Bloomsbury Publishing Plc

First published 2013

British Library Cataloguing-in-Publication Data
A catalogue record for this book is available from the British Library.

ISBN: PB: 978-1-4725-3118-6
ePub: 978-1-4725-2601-4
ePDF: 978-1-4725-3384-5

Library of Congress Cataloging-in-Publication Data
A catalog record for this book is available from the Library of Congress.

Typeset by Mark Heslington Ltd, Scarborough, North Yorkshire
Printed and bound in Great Britain

The Grand Gesture

The Grand Gesture, freely adapted by Deborah McAndrew from *The Suicide* by Nikolai Erdman was originally produced by Northern Broadsides in partnership with Harrogate Theatre. The first performance was on 6 September 2013 at Harrogate Theatre with the following cast and creatives:

Simeon Duff (our hero)	**Michael Hugo**
Mary Duff (his wife)	**Samantha Robinson**
Sadie (her mother)	**Angela Bain**
Al Bush (their landlord)	**Howard Chadwick**
Maggie Johnson (landlady of *The Blind Piper* public house)	**Claire Storey**
George Timms (a Marxist postman)	**Paul Barnhill**
Victor Stark (an intellectual)	**Robert Pickavance**
Father MacLeod (a Catholic priest)	**Alan McMahon**
Nicholas Pugh (a businessman)	**Dyfrig Morris**
Chloe MacSween (rival in love)	**Sophia Hatfield**
Rosie Philpot (rival in love)	**Hester Arden**

The location is a port in the North West of England

Director	**Conrad Nelson**
Designer	**Dawn Allsopp**
Lighting Designer	**Mark Howland**
Musical Director	**Rebekah Hughes**
Production Manager	**Kay Burnett**
Company Stage Manager (and on the book)	**Katie Bevan**
Technical Manager	**Adam Foley**
Wardrobe Supervisor	**Katie Worfolk**
Assistant Stage Manager	**Suzanne Snook**
Production Photography	**Nobby Clark**
Translation Consultant	**Marianna K Ivanova**
Marketing	**The Experience Business**
Press	**Duncan Clarke PR**
Executive Director	**Sue Andrews**
Artistic Director & Founder	**Barrie Rutter**
Financial Administrator	**Alex Kilburn**

Characters

Simeon Duff, *our hero*
Mary Duff, *his wife*
Sadie, *her mother*
Al Bush, *their landlord*
Maggie Johnson, *landlady of* The Blind Piper *public house*
George Timms, *a Marxist postman*
Victor Stark, *an intellectual*
Chloe MacSween, *rival in love*
Nicholas Pugh, *a businessman*
Father MacLeod, *a Catholic priest*
Rosie Philpot, *rival in love*

Cast will double, where required, and appear as **Gypsy Band**, **Choir** *and* **Undertakers**.

The location is a city port in the North West of England – with a blend of Lancashire, Liverpool, Welsh, Scots and Irish voices.

Songs are marked **Traditional** *for existing folk songs and* **Original** *for new song lyrics requiring musical composition.*

Fiddlers' Green *is used by kind permission of John Conolly.*

Act One

A dystopian world.

The innards of a decaying boarding house.

Bearing no relation to how they might be placed in reality: a double bed; a small table, with a drawer; doors; a window.

Music.

Three **Gypsy Women** *enter.*

Gypsies (*sing*) **The Ballad of Simeon Duff (Original)**

O hear the ballad of Simeon Duff.
Life was hard and he'd had enough,
Money was tight as a hamster's chuff –
For Simeon, Simeon Duff.

The world was cruel to Simeon Duff.
Mad and mired in the deepest slough.
Nobody seemed to give a stuff –
'Bout Simeon, Simeon Duff.

And when it seemed he had no choice
This voiceless man,
With debts piled high and bills unpaid,
He made a plan.

No more picking at navel fluff.
Problem solved with a pinch of snuff,
He said he'd do it – they called his bluff!
O Simeon, Simeon Duff.
O Simeon, Simeon, one in a million Simeon, Simeon Duff.

Blackout.

Voices in the darkness.

Simeon (*soft*)   Mary. Mary, are you asleep? (*Loud.*) Mary!

Mary (*jumps out of her skin*)   Ah!

Simeon   What's up? What's up?

Mary   Someone's shouting.

Simeon   Me.

Mary   You.

Simeon   Me. I wanted to ask . . . I know it's late, an' all . . . Only I was lying here wondering, Mary . . . Mary? Mary, are you asleep? (*Loud.*) Mary!

Mary (*jumps out of her skin*)   Ah!

Simeon   What's up? What's up?

Mary   Someone's shouting.

Simeon   Me.

Mary   You.

Simeon   Me again.

Mary   What do you want, Simeon?

Simeon   I was wondering if you saved me a sausage?

Mary   A what?

Simeon   The sausage left over from tea. Did you save it?

Mary   Are you having me on? You woke me up to ask if I saved you a sausage?

Simeon   Yes.

Mary   A bloody sausage?

Simeon   A banger.

Mary   Have you any idea what time it is, Simeon? I've got to be up for work at the crack o' dawn. Work Simeon, work. The daily grind; blinding, mind-bogglingly boring bloody work. And at the end of every day my head's banging like a boghouse door in a force ten, my back's broke in four places and my feet look like a bag of freakin' walnuts. I'm ragged with it, Simeon, and if I don't get eight hours I'll crack up. And just because you can't sleep . . .

Simeon (*a gentle snore*)

Mary   Simeon?

Simeon (*a gentle snore*)

Mary   Are you asleep? (*Loud.*) Simeon!

Simeon (*jumps out of his skin*)   Ah!

Mary   What's up? What's up?

Simeon   Someone's shouting.

Mary   Me.

Simeon   You.

Mary   Me.

Simeon   What do you want, Mary?

Mary   I don't want anything. You wanted a sausage.

Simeon   Did you get it?

Mary   No. No I didn't.

Simeon   Are you going now?

Mary   No I'm not, so will you stop gobbing on and go to sleep!

In the dark we hear the bad tempered punching of pillows and general 'trying to get comfortable' acting.

A moment of silence.

Mary (*sigh of frustration*)   I'm wide awake now. You've done me in – you and your sausage. Why didn't you eat it at tea-time, eh? Me and Mam cooked it 'specially for you – your favourite, bangers and mash. I gave you the biggest plate an' all.

Simeon   And why d'you do that, eh? I know, don't I. To humiliate me. Because I haven't earned it. You have. You're the one that's working. Only I get the extra sausage. Is that supposed to make me feel important? Well it doesn't. It's a flagrant and injurious attack on the very quintessence of my manhood. That sausage is a psychological sausage.

Mary   Right. Right. Never let it be said . . . Where's the light?

A click. Nothing.

Fused again.

Simeon   Or the landlord hasn't paid the leccy.

Mary   I've got the candle.

Simeon   Leave it, Mary.

Mary   Where's the matches?

Simeon   I've gone past it.

Mary   You were famished.

Simeon   Peckish.

Mary   Starved.

Simeon   I don't want it.

Mary   You're having it.

She strikes a match – a flare in the dark and the glow of a candle, illuminating two weary young faces.

God's sake, Simeon, life's hard enough without fighting over a bit of sausage. Do you want a dollop of cold mash to go with it? Slice of bread? Make a sarnie.

Simeon   I don't want mash, or bread. I'm not eating it.

Mary   Why not?

Simeon   Because I'd have to swallow a flamin' sermon along with it.

Mary   Have I said anything?

Simeon   I can see it on your face. Contempt. You've no respect for me any more, and why should you? I've no respect for myself. You work hard – but it's far worse for me. I don't work at all. It affects a man, in all kinds of ways . . .

Mary   I've told before I'm not bothered about that.

Simeon   And now, to cap it all, I've started to get nervous symptoms.

Mary   What?

Simeon   Look –

He throws back the covers of the bed – he is wearing t-shirt and shorts. He crosses his legs and bangs the reflex point on his knee with the side of his hand. A beat late, his leg flies up in the air and becomes rigid.

See that. I used to have cat reflexes. I was a like a lynx. Now I'm more like a three-toed sloth on a mobility scooter. How am I supposed to get a job with a twitch like that?

Mary   They might have you in the circus, I suppose.

Simeon   Is that meant to be funny?

Mary   You've got a bit of a twitch, that's all!

Simeon   That's all? That's all! I'm falling apart here and you're laughing at me. What you trying to do to me? Tip me over the edge, eh? I'll tell you what, Mary – there might be only one way into this world – but there's plenty of ways to go out –

Mary   Well do us all a favour then, you miserable get. Be one less mouth to feed.

Simeon   And the truth comes out –

Mary   I didn't mean it /

Simeon   You wish I were dead /

Mary   I don't /

Simeon   What do you recommend? Rope, dagger, lead pipe? Shall I shoot myself?

Mary   You haven't got a gun.

Simeon   You don't know what I've got.

Mary   Where is it then? Eh? Go on, Simeon – where's the revolver?

Simeon   You bloody cow.

Mary   Simeon!

Simeon   Heartless bitch!

With a cry of shock, **Mary** *lets the candle drop.*

Blackout.

Mary   Sim . . . Sim, don't speak to me like that. I'm sorry, love – but you push me too far sometimes. Where are you? Come here. Let's make up, eh? Speak to me, Simeon . . . Why won't you speak to me? Come on, eh . . . Tell you what, I'll go get you that sausage – (*Warm.*) or . . . hows about I put my coat and slippers on, and nip out for a nice pasty from the all night garage . . . ?

Sadie (*Irish*)   No thanks.

Mary   Mother?

Sadie   What's all the feckin' row, Mary Duff? A person can't get any sleep with all this crashing and shouting and malarky. And the lights are out again, so we're all in the pitch and there's nothing to do but sleep, and you'll be wakin' everyone in the feckin' building. Well? Are you not speaking?

Mary   No.

Sadie   Well that's grand. So, Simeon – are you going to tell me what's going on? Simeon Duff, I'm asking you a question.

Mary   Don't ask him, Mam. He's got a right monk on.

Sadie   That right, Simeon?

Mary   He's not speaking either.

Sadie   And here's me thought he was miming.

Mary   Simeon, answer my mother when she speaks to you . . .

Sadie   He is all right, I suppose.

Mary   Well . . . he . . . he was quite upset.

Sadie   In what way?

Mary   Threatening to shoot himself . . .

Sadie   What?

Mary   It was a joke. He wasn't serious . . . Simeon, say something. I'm worried now. Please. Sim . . . ?

Sadie   What you doing, Mary?

Mary   I'm looking for him. He was on the bed.

Sadie   Has he fallen out?

Mary   I can't find him. Light the candle, Mam.

Sadie   Oh, this is fine, in the middle of the night – in the pitch – with Simeon Duff playing silly-feckers . . .

Mary   Get the candle, mother. I dropped it on the floor somewhere round the bed. Simeon, you're scaring me – please say something.

Sadie   I'm on my hands and knees, I can't find it.

Mary   I was round the side, by the cheese plant.

A crash, a scream!

What was that?

Sadie   The cheese plant.

Mary   Simeon, this isn't funny – I'm really worried now.

Sadie (*muttering*)   'Holy St Anthony, who received from God the special power of restoring lost things, grant that . . .'

Mary   What are you doing, mother?

Sadie   Novena – hush now . . . 'grant that I may find the candle which has been lost / . . .'

Mary   I've got it!

Sadie   Thanks be to blessed Saint Anthony. Now – how about the matches, Lord? (*Mutters again.*) 'Holy Saint Anthony / . . .'

Mary   Matches are on the side table. Quickly, Mam!

Sadie   I'm doing my best.

Mary   Oh Simeon, Simeon . . .

Match is struck, candle glow revealing **Mary** *and* **Sadie**, *but no* **Simeon**.

Sadie   Where is he?

Mary   He's gone. Oh, Mam. He was desperate. He was . . . Oh God, he was in a right old state. Where's my skirt?

Sadie   What?

Mary   I'm going to find him.

Sadie   He can't have gone far.

Mary   He's not in his right mind. He showed me his twitch.

Sadie   Mother of God!

Mary   My skirt, where's my skirt?

Sadie   Is this it?

Mary   That's Simeon's trousers.

Sadie   Praised be Blessed Saint Agnes of Bohemia.

Mary What?

Sadie If his pants are here, he can't have gone far, can he.

Mary He could have gone out without them.

Sadie No – as we say at home – a man without pants is like a man marooned.

Mary So where is he then?

Sadie Probably just popped to the little boys' room – you know . . .

Mary And what's to stop him doing something drastic in there?

Sadie Oh, don't be so melodramatic, Mary Angelica Duff. What could he possibly find to top himself with in the bathroom, eh – apart from a rusty razor? Sure, there's a bathtub – but you'd need to run it ever so deep to drown. And we're only on the third floor so if he fancied jumping he'd have to go down head first to make a job of it. Mind, it's just as well that the lights are out or he might spot that good stout hook on the back of the door . . .

Mary Oh God . . .

Mary *runs out in distress.*

Sadie (*crossing herself*) Blessed Mother, Our Lady of Knock, Walsingham, Lourdes, Fatima, Medjugorje and Guadalupe – Lady of Sorrows intercede with your Blessed son, our Lord, on behalf of Simeon Duff – who has flipped his tiddlywink into Satan's stewpot and succumbed to the mortal sin of despair . . .

Mary *returns.*

Mary He's in there. He's locked the door.

Sadie Did you talk to him? What's he doing?

Mary He wouldn't answer. Oh, Mam – he could be dying in there.

Sadie   Or having a pee.

Mary   I'm going to get Al.

Sadie   You can't wake Mr Bush.

Mary   He could break down the door.

Sadie   But he's only just lost his wife. The poor man is in deepest mourning.

Mary   And he won't be the only one if we don't get to Simeon in time.

Sadie   You'd better knock him up. I'll light another candle.

Mary   No – you'll go and stand by the bathroom door and try and talk him round. He said he had a gun!

Sadie   Jesus, Mary and Joseph!

Mary *grabs the candle and runs to a door.*

Sadie *heads off in the darkness in the direction of the bathroom.*

Mary *knocking and stage whispering.*

Mary   Mr Bush! Al, are you there?

Enter **Al** *through the door.*

Al *and* **Mary** *lit by her candle.*

Al   What's up? Who's that?

Mary   It's me – Mary Duff.

Al   Good evening, Mary.

Mary   Good evening, Al.

Al   Good night.

Mary   Al! Wait!

Al   Will you keep the bloody noise down.

Mary   Please, Al. I need you. I need a man.

Al I'm very flattered, Mary – but your husband might have something to say about that?

Mary My husband's not saying anything.

Al Take a cold shower.

Mary But he's in the bathroom.

Al Then wait your turn.

Mary He's demoralised.

Al I'm busy.

Mary I'm desperate.

Al Not tonight, Mary Duff.

Al closes the door and *Mary's candle is blown out.*

Darkness.

Mary Please, Mr Bush. I need you.
  It's an emergency!
  I'll break down the door.

Door opens, revealing **Maggie Johnson** – *in nightwear, carrying a torch, which lights her and* **Mary**.

Maggie Do you mind!

Mary Maggie?

Maggie Bit fresh, aren't you? Coming onto a grieving widower in the midst of his anguish.

Mary What are you doing here?

Maggie Consoling Mr Bush, who was just pouring his broken heart into a hot mug of Horlicks, when you come, threatening to break down his door – you trollop.

Mary Not *his* door. The bathroom!

Maggie Young women nowadays! You've got one-track minds.

Enter **Al**.

Al   Maggie love, if you're planning to crack her one, will you take her outside. I don't want the Bizzies round here again.

Maggie   Am I supposed to stand by then, while other women throw themselves at you in the middle of the night?

Mary   Excuse me – I'm a married woman!

Maggie   So what? So am I.

Mary   But I'll be a widow any minute, if we don't get to him in time.

Al   What are you on about, Mary Duff?

Mary   Simeon. He's barricaded himself into the bog and he's going to blow his own brains out.

Al   He's got a gun?

Mary   Please, Al. I need you to break the door down.

Al   Why didn't you say so?

Al *springs into action with* **Mary** *and* **Maggie** *in pursuit. They are intercepted by* **Sadie**.

Sadie   Stop! Don't do it. Oh Jeannie Mac, what a shock I've had.

Mary   Are we too late!

Sadie   I went to the bathroom door, and I looked through the keyhole. The silvery moonlight flooded the room – what a sight!

Mary   Oh dear God.

Sadie   It was George Timms – waving his auld feller about like a 'lympic torch. I've never seen the like.

Enter **George** – *carrying an Army Surplus style camping lantern.*

George   Evening.

They are all speechless at the thought of his 'lympic torch.

Bathroom's free.

Beat.

Might want to . . . give it a minute . . .

George *exits.*

Mary   Oh Simeon. Where can he be?

Al   Have you searched the whole house?

Mary   It's not easy you know, what with the leccy going off again.

Maggie   He must have gone out.

Sadie   With no pants on?

Mary   A man staring into the abyss has no need of pants.

Maggie   That's true enough.

Sadie   Look on the bright side. If he is wandering the town with his auld feller hanging out, he'll probably be arrested before he gets chance to kill himself.

Mary *lets out a wail of distress.*

Al   Could he still be in the house?

Sadie   What about the kitchen – he could be at the knife drawer.

Al   Right – come on, Mary. You two stay here.

Al *and* **Mary** *exit.*

Maggie   Huh. Typical. I know his game. If Simeon's topped himself, Al Bush'll be the first on the scene to 'comfort' the grieving widow.

Sadie   But he's only just lost his wife.

Maggie   So there's a gap in his diary.

Off – a scream from **Mary** *and loud crack and a dull thud.*

Sadie   Oh God! It's over. It's all over. I may scream. Should I scream? Will it help? I don't know. (*Sharp intake of breath . . .*)

Maggie   Don't.

Sadie   The poor man. Simeon Duff – a spineless sack o' shite, but a man for all that . . .

Maggie   Oh God – do you think they'll bring him up here?

Sadie   Why would they do that if he's dead?

Maggie   He might just be horribly injured.

Sadie   I don't like blood. I could never have been a surgeon.

Enter **Al**, *dragging* **Simeon** *– who is wearing a tatty dressing gown, over his t-shirt and shorts.*

Simeon   Let go of me! What do you think you're doing?

Al   Calm down, Simeon, calm down.

Simeon   Let me go.

Al   Mrs O'Toole – you need to go see to Mary.

Sadie   Dear God, he shot her.

Al   She's fainted. Out cold on the kitchen floor.

Sadie   Saints preserve us!

Exit **Sadie**.

Al   Maggie. You got a nip of something there?

Maggie *pulls a whisky flask from her dressing gown pocket and exits after* **Sadie**.

Al   Now, Simeon Duff. Let's see what you've got in your pockets, eh?

A struggle, as **Al** *tries to feel* **Simeon***'s dressing gown pockets – they move towards the bedroom space*

Simeon   What the bloody hell do you think you're doing?

Al   Give it to me, Simeon.

Simeon   I beg your pardon.

Al   I want it. You're going to give it to me.

Simeon   Mr Bush – that's not really my thing, you know . . .

Al   The gun, Simeon. Where's the gun?

Simeon   The what?

Al   I saw you. You were sticking it in your mouth.

Simeon   A gun?

Al   No point denying it. I don't know how you got hold of it, but you have to give it up, Simeon.

Simeon   I don't know what you're talking about. Let go of me!

Al   All right. I'll let go – but you must promise to hear me out, before you do anything rash.

Simeon   OK. (*Beat.*) OK!

Al *releases* **Simeon**. *They regard each other suspiciously.*

Through the past few minutes of action, dawn has broken and the stage is filling with a grey, early light . . . Now we see the shabbiness of the house, the unmade bed and the broken cheese plant.

Three **Gypsy Women** *enter, carrying yellow flowers, playing birdsong on a flute.*

Al   Hear that?

The **Gypsies** *pass through the space and place the flowers in the room, as sunlight floods the stage.*

Al   See. Even after the blackest night – the light returns.

Gypsies *hum an intro to* **Morning Has Broken (Traditional)**

Al The sun's coming up . . .

Simeon So what?

Al (*sings*) Morning has broken like the first morning.

Blackbird has spoken, like the first bird.

Gypsies (*sing*) Praise for the singing, praise for the morning . . .

Praise for them springing fresh from the word.

Sing/hum next verse under the dialogue.

Al Simeon – the day has dawned. The dark night of the soul is over. Look, Simeon. Look out of the window. See the birds, the sun, the sky. Life is beautiful.

Simeon Is it?

Al The best things in life are free, Simeon.

Simeon Except food, and drink, and heating and lights!

Al You must count your blessings. The world is full of wonder.

Simeon The world is spinning off into the future and leaving me behind at the wrong side of town, in a rundown house, in a rented room.

Al It's a rough patch, that's all. When you get a job /

Simeon What job? There are no bloody jobs.

Al Mary's working.

Simeon And that's supposed to make me feel better, is it?

Al You have to struggle in this life, Simeon.

Simeon Struggle?

Singing stops.

Simeon   God Almighty, Al – do you think I haven't tried? I've done it all – programmes, placements, jobmatch, jobsearch, oddjob, bobajob, bad job, blow job /

Al   You what?

Simeon   Jobseeker, that's me. Seeker of jobs. I've done more interviews than you've had barmaids – and with more style. Smart, casual; smiley, serious; confident, curious; macho, metro – I even wore a touch of eyeliner on the last one I went for. And here I am, still on the Scratch. They've told me I have to be prepared to consider any career path open to me . . . That's when I found this . . .

He pulls a battered pamphlet out of one of his pockets and hands it to **Al**.

Al   'Blow your own. How to play the tuba in ten easy lessons with Theodore Hugo Shultz.'

Simeon   I could do that.

Al   Play the tuba?

Simeon   It's a good life, a musician. No shortage of bands round here either, and musos have a good union and that. Get proper pay – like fifty quid an hour, or something. I've done the sums – see . . . (*Takes a scrap of paper out his other pocket.*) Three or four gigs a week – that's eight to ten a month, probably more round Christmas, so let's say over a hundred a year. Gotta be at least two hours per gig . . . I'm looking at – well, work it out for yourself.

Al   But don't you have to study for years . . .

Simeon   How hard can it be, eh? Says here – ten easy lessons. It's not about study, it's about privilege.

Al   What do you mean?

Simeon   I mean, I've got the desire, I've got the brains – and I've got the book. The only thing I need is the tuba. But they cost a fortune. There's the rub, see? Privilege. I can't afford it.

Al   So you think a tuba is the answer to all your problems?

Simeon   I'm certain of it.

Al   And if you could only get hold of an instrument your troubles would be over?

Simeon   They would.

Al   Cling to that dream, Simeon. Cherish it, nourish it – and all will be well.

Simeon   It will.

Music intro to final verse . . .

Al   There is hope now. A vision of the future. Bigger. Better. Brassier. Oh Simeon, you have such a lot to live for.

Simeon   I do. I do. I really do.

Gypsies (*sing*)   Mine is the sunlight, mine is the morning
   Born of the one light Eden saw play.

Simeon   The tuba.

Al   The tuba. Music is the answer.

All (*sing*)   Praise with elation, praise every morning
   God's recreation of the new day.

*The **Gypsy Singers** melt away.*

Al   So, give me the gun.

Simeon   What gun?

Al   You don't need it now.

Simeon   Who said I had a gun.

Al   Mary.

Simeon   Oh did she.

Al   It's understandable, Simeon. We all know how you feel – but now you have something to live for. You don't need to shoot yourself any more.

Simeon   Why would I want to shoot myself?

Al   No reason at all – at least, not any more. We know it's been hard for you, Simeon, basically living off your wife's wage all this time – it can't have been easy. And what with your mother-in-law to look after an' all. God knows, that woman'd drive me to it on her own, without the added humiliation of being unemployed all these months, and no real hope of finding another job. We're all very sorry for you, Simeon.

Simeon   Humilation.

Al   Indignity. Belittlement.

Simeon   Disgrace.

Al   You feel ashamed. Everyone knows it.

Simeon   Do they now.

Al   But you've turned the corner. A new day has dawned.

Simeon   Sod off, Al. You hear me? Do one!

Al   Give me the gun, Simeon.

Simeon   For the last time, I haven't got a bloody gun. Where would I get a gun, eh?

Al   It's not that hard these days, you know it.

Simeon   Do I?

Al   I think we both know that Marko the Russian can get hold of pretty much anything.

Simeon   Pawnbroker's on Market Street?

Al   Raided last week. They didn't find anything, but since then he's been offloading all kinds of gear . . .

Simeon   I didn't know that.

Al   Course you didn't. Now – give – me – the –

Al *lunges at* **Simeon** *to grab him, but* **Simeon** *wriggles free and points something at* **Al** *through the pocket of his dressing gown.*

Simeon   Get away from me!

Al   Now, Simeon . . .

Simeon   Get out. Out! Or I'll shoot myself right here, right now, right in front of you.

Al   You wouldn't.

Simeon   Ashamed, am I? Humiliated, am I?

Al   Life is beautiful.

Simeon   You can't eat life, Al. Beauty doesn't pay the rent.

Al (*sings*)   Morning has broken . . .

Simeon   Shut up. Shut up. Shut up! *I'm* broken. *I'm* broken.

Al   You don't really want to shoot yourself, Simeon.

Simeon   Oh yeah? Wanna bet? In three!

Al   Don't . . .

Simeon   One!

Al   Please . . .

Simeon   Two!

Al   Oh God!

Al *exits hurriedly.*

Simeon   Three . . .

Simeon *pulls a large sausage from his pocket and takes a bite. Chews. Swallows.*

Bang!

Humiliated. Ashamed. Worthless. Everybody's talking about me, are they? Sorry for me – living off my wife? What's she been saying about me, eh? All right then . . .

He pulls the wedding ring off his finger.

She might as well pay for everything.

He exits one way, as **Al** *tentatively enters by another.*

Al   Simeon . . . ? I just want to help. I truly believe that in spite of everything you could still see how beautiful life is . . . Simeon?

Maggie *and* **Sadie** *enter, carrying an unconscious* **Mary**.

Maggie   She doesn't look this heavy when she's upright, does she?

Sadie   She's always been a good eater.

Maggie   I suppose it's the dead weight.

Sadie   Don't say 'dead', Maggie Johnson. Not under the present circumstances.

Maggie   Are you going to stand there gawping, Al Bush, or are you going to give us a hand.

Sadie   Just get her onto the bed.

They dump **Mary** *unceremoniously on the bed and survey the situation.*

Sadie   Loosen her clothes.

Al *steps forward and is pulled back by* **Maggie**.

Maggie   Easy tiger.

Mary   Oh, oh . . .

Al   She's coming round.

Sadie   Oh, Mary darlin' – you're with us once again. Thanks be to Saint Kenneth – who ran to pray for the deliverance of Saint Columba wearing only one shoe.

Mary   Simeon? Darling, Sim, where are you?

Sadie   Don't you worry, Mary. Simeon's fine. Al Bush has got him under control.

The three women all look at **Al**.

Maggie   Well?

Sadie   Where'd he go?

Mary   Oh God. He's dead isn't he? He did it – he shot himself.

Al   No, Mrs Duff. To the best of my knowledge he's not dead. Yet.

Mary   We have to find him.

Al   That might do more harm than good. He threatened to shoot himself in front of me right there and then. I tried to reason with him, I thought I had him, but he's depressed.

Sadie   We'll have a Mass.

Maggie   Never mind calling on the Lord. We need to call the police. Have him arrested.

Al   What for? There's no law against trying to kill yourself. A person can't be tried and sentenced to 'live'

Mary   Is there no way we can save him?

Al   There may be a way . . .

Women   Yes?

Al   Though I don't know how we'd do it . . .

Women   Yes?

Al   But the key to it all is . . .

Women   Yes?

Al   . . . the horn.

Mary   Don't you think I've tried that?

Al   A tuba.

Maggie   A tuba?

Al   Simeon thinks that music is the answer to all his problems.

Sadie   I'll get onto Saint Cecilia right away.

Mary   How much does one of these things cost?

Maggie   A basic instrument'll set you back a grand or more . . .

Mary   A thousand pounds! If we had that kind of money Simeon wouldn't need to learn the bloody tuba!

Sadie   You seem to be awful well informed about horns, Maggie Johnson?

Maggie   A lot of musicians perform at my pub. One of them is a brass player.

Al   Do you think they'd lend Simeon a horn – to get him started?

Maggie   No harm in asking.

Sadie   You'd better get a shifty on, or it'll be too feckin' late.

Mary   But we can't be disturbing people at this hour.

Maggie   They're musicians. If we're quick enough we'll catch 'em just before they go to bed. Come on, chuck.

Maggie *and* **Mary** *exit.*

Sadie (*calling after*)   You might wanna get dressed first, Maggie Johnson.

Al   It's a bad business this, missus.

Sadie   You don't think he'll last until they get the horn?

Al   We don't even know where he is.

Sadie   What'll we do?

Al   I'll go and look for him. You wait here, in case he shows up.

Sadie   And what use am I, if he does?

Al   Just keep him talking.

Sadie   What about?

Al   How should I know. You're Irish, aren't you?

Sadie   In what sense?

Al   Blarney. You're supposed to have the gift – as a nation.

Sadie   That's an awful stereotype, Al Bush. I never had any such gift. The only thing my mother gave me was beauty.

Al   Did she never tell you stories? About the little folk and the fair Colleens, and the Celtic Kings?

Sadie   She once saw the face of Saint Patrick in a plate of colcannon mash.

Al   That'll do. A funny story.

Sadie   What's funny about it? Saint Pat glaring up at you – with a fork up his nose. It'd put you right off.

Al   Mrs O'Toole – your son-in-law is in desperate peril. And I know you'll do whatever it takes to keep him this side of the grave until we can find that tuba. Amuse him, inspire him, distract him.

Sadie   Do you have faith in me, Al?

Al   Mrs O'Toole. Sadie. I do.

Exit **Al**.

Sadie *kneels by the bed and crosses herself.*

Sadie   Now then, Lord. This is quite specific. I've no idea what saint you pray to for saving sons-in-law from self-destruction in time to learn to play the tuba . . .

Enter **Simeon**.

Sadie *ducks down – unseen*

Simeon *takes a revolver from his pocket and places it on the small table. Removes a pad of paper and pen from the table draw and begins to write.*

Simeon   In the event of my death . . .

Sadie   Oh Lord! Don't do it, Simeon.

Simeon   Mother! You nearly scared me to death. I wish you had. You'd have saved me a job.

Sadie   You don't want to leave this world, Simeon – this world full of miracles and wonders.

Simeon   No miracles any more, Mother.

Sadie   Sure there is. Did I never tell you the story about my dear old mam and the vision she had of Saint Patrick?

Simeon   No, you didn't.

Sadie   I just chanced to recall it a moment ago. It was the mash, you see. It must have landed, just so, onto the plate – and there he was . . .

Simeon   Mash?

Sadie   Colcannon. Steamy and lovely. She'd made a hole in the middle see, for the butter – I suppose that must have looked like a mouth – or perhaps a nostril . . . and there he was.

Simeon   Who?

Sadie   Saint Patrick.

Simeon   And?

Sadie   It was the living spit of him.

Simeon   And?

Sadie   Well, that's it.

Simeon   That's it.

Beat – **Sadie** *is desperate.*

Sadie (*sings*)   **Colcannon (Traditional)**

> Did you ever eat Colcannon,
> Made from lovely pickled cream?

Simeon   What?

Sadie   With the greens and scallions mingled
Like a picture in a dream.

Enter three **Gypsies**, *carrying pots and pans that they play in rhythm.*

> Did you ever make a hole on top
> To hold the melting flake
> Of the creamy, flavoured butter
> That your mother used to make?

Simeon   Get out, Sadie!

Sadie   No, Simeon – I'm supposed to distract you, or amuse you – or something . . . Did you never eat colcannon?

Simeon   No. Never. Never in my life!

Sadie *and* **Gypsies** (*sing*)   Yes you did, so you did, so did he and so did I.
And the more I think about it sure the nearer I'm to cry.
Oh, wasn't it the happy days when troubles we knew not,
And our mothers made colcannon in the little skillet pot.

Simeon   Leave me alone. I don't want company or help –

Sadie   But you were happy once, Simeon. Think on that. Remember. You had dreams of something better . . .

Simeon   I never had any dreams!

He chases **Sadie** *off.*

Simeon   Never! You hear me? I never had any dreams!

Gypsies (*sing*)   Yes you did, so you did, so did he and so did I.

And the more I think about it sure the nearer I'm to cry.
    . . .

Simeon *returns to the table and writes.*

Simeon   In the event of my death . . .

Gypsies   Oh, wasn't it the happy days when troubles we had not . . .

Simeon   In the event of my death, I blame no one.

Act Two

Later that day.

The scene as in Act I, but tidied up and objects moved in relation to each other.

The doors are in different places too – to become other doors.

Simeon *seated, with a tuba and the tuition pamphlet.*

Mary *and* **Sadie** *in attendance – drinking tea from cups and saucers.*

Simeon (*reads*) 'Blow your own. How to play the tuba in ten easy lessons with Theodore Hugo Shultz. Chapter one – getting to grips with your tuba. Place the first finger of your right hand on the valve nearest to your mouth-piece; middle finger on the second valve; fourth finger on the third valve.' OK . . . So far so good. 'Without pressing any valves, the note sounded will be C . . .'

He blows into the tuba – no sound.

Blows again – no sound.

Blows again – so hard he nearly hyperventilates – no sound.

Flamin' hell, our Mary, I nearly passed out then. What's up with it?

Sadie   It must be broke.

Mary   What does it say in the book?

Simeon *consults the pamphlet.*

Simeon   Ah – 'How to blow – the Shultz method. For this purpose you will first require a piece of tissue paper . . .'

Mary   Tissue. Mam, do we have any tissue?

Sadie   No. Wait – how about that scratchy, arse-busting bog roll?

Simeon   Get it.

Sadie *exits.*

Mary   What does it say next, Simeon?

Simeon   'In order to develop the correct oral positioning and blowing technique for the tuba, Theodore Hugo Shultz recommends that you take a small piece of the tissue paper . . .'

Sadie *returns at a rush with the toilet tissue.*

'. . . and place it on the tongue.'

Simeon, *undaunted, eyeballs* **Sadie** *and puts out his tongue. She approaches and places a piece of tissue paper on his tongue.*

Mary   Now what?

Simeon   Ea e ex i or ee.

Mary   What?

Simeon   I ai – ou ea e ex i or ee.

Mary/Sadie   What?

Simeon *spits out paper.*

Simeon   I said – you read the next bit for me.

Mary   Oh – right.

Mary *takes pamphlet, while* **Sadie** *applies another piece of toilet paper to* **Simeon**'s *tongue.*

Mary   'Theodore Hugo Shultz recommends . . . small piece . . . on the tongue . . .' Ah, here we are . . . '. . . and then spit the paper onto the floor.'

Simeon *spits.*

Simeon   I just did that! I just bloody did it!

Mary   'After spitting, try and hold the exact position of the mouth and then blow into the tuba.'

Furious beat.

Sadie   Now – don't get downhearted, Simeon . . .

Simeon *sticks out his tongue again for tissue to be again applies by* **Sadie**.

In one fluid movement he spits, inhales, blows – a beautiful B-flat sounds.

Triumph.

Sadie   Oh thank God, thank God!

Simeon   I did it! Right – get pen and paper, Mary. You're writing your letter of resignation. Better still – don't bother going in to work ever again. This is our ticket back to black.

Mary   I'll have to keep working for a while yet.

Simeon   I'll have this off in no time.

Sadie   You've still got to learn, Simeon.

Simeon   You've just seen me do it, Mother. The biggest part is knowing how to spit, and I've got that down already. Listen.

He blows again into the tuba – a beautiful, sonorous note.

We're on our way up now, Mary. This horn is our fortune. I've got it all worked out . . . (*Takes a piece of paper from his pocket.*) 'In the event of my death . . .' Hold on, that's not it . . . (*Throws it down and takes out another piece of paper.*) There, see – three or four gigs a week – eight to ten a month . . . Work it out for yourself, Mary. It's a golden ticket.

Mary   Oh, Simeon.

Simeon   We'll have the best of everything now, you'll see. Move out of these crappy digs into a spanking new house with a granny flat for Mother. You'll have designer clobber and get your hair done at Salon Geoffrey – and when I come in late from a gig, you'll have my favourite tipple waiting for me . . .

Mary   Egg flip?

Simeon   Egg flip.

Sadie   Ooh – I love an egg flip.

Mary   But that's ever so expensive to make – eggs, cream, brandy . . .

Simeon   We can afford it. Every night of the week if we feel like it.

Sadie   That tuba is a feckin' miracle.

Simeon   Silence, Mother! I need total silence while I practice my music. (*Blows a confident note to consolidate his learning and delight the women.*) OK. The next chapter is entitled 'The Scale'.

Mary/Sadie   The scale. The scale. The scale.

Simeon   Here we go. (*Reads.*) 'The scale is the skeleton of music. Once you have mastered the scale you can start to build and flex your musical muscles . . .'

Sadie   Do you get a belly button?

Simeon   What?

Sadie   Just wondering, if you get bones and body bits, do you get a belly button?

Simeon   What's musical about a belly button?

Sadie   What's musical about muscles?

Simeon   It's an analogy.

Sadie   How can you have an allergy to belly buttons?

Simeon   Will you stop distracting me.

Mary   Quiet, Mother!

Simeon   Where was I? (*Reads.*) 'The scale . . . skeleton of music . . .'

Sadie (*sideways to* **Mary**) I knew a man back home who played the bones – (*Mouths.*) beautiful.

Simeon 'In order to learn the scale properly, Theodore Hugo Shultz recommends the following method. First, play the scale on your . . . (*Turns page.*) piano . . .' (*Beat.*) Must have turned two pages at once. (*Turns back.*) 'First, play the scale on your . . . (*Turns page.*) piano!

Sadie Did you get a piano as well, Simeon Duff?

Simeon Of course I bloody didn't.

Mary Where would we get a piano from?

Simeon A piano!

Mary They're even dearer than tubas!

Simeon *tears up the pamphlet.*

Simeon Theodore Hugo Shultz – world famous musician – world famous fraud – him and his bloody belly button!

Mary Oh Simeon, try not to be too disappointed.

Simeon This was my Holy grail. My horn of plenty. My future.

Sadie Well – never mind. It'd be a devil to clean.

Mary We'll be OK.

Simeon Who'll be OK? You? Me? I won't be OK. I'm nothing, me. Nothing. A no-mark.

Mary We've managed 'til now – we'll just keep going.

Simeon On your wage . . . ?

Sadie And the prayers of the Blessed Virgin.

Simeon Who bought these cups?

Mary You did.

Simeon   That's right. Me. When I had a job we could afford to buy stuff – like pots and glasses. I bought them, but we're 'OK' on just your wage, Mary. So it won't matter when things get broken, will it?

Mary   No.

Simeon   We can afford new things, on just your wage – can't we?

Mary   Yes, of course.

Simeon   Of course.

He throws a cup to the ground, breaking it.

Mary   What you doing?

Simeon   I bought that. But you can afford to replace it, so that's 'OK'.

Mary   No, it's not.

Simeon   Oh really?

He picks up the saucer

Mary   Please, Simeon. Stop it. We can't afford it.

Simeon   Can't we? Well in that case . . . (*Places the saucer back on the table, carefully.*) Get out. If you can't afford a cup and saucer, you can't afford me!

Mary   Of course I can, Sim. There's enough for all three of us.

Simeon   Oh. Right then – (*Picks up saucer and smashes it.*)

Sadie (*sorrowful*)   O – he's mad as a mushroom.

Simeon *screams.*

Mary *screams.*

Simeon *screams.*

Mary *screams.*

Simeon *smashes the other cup.*

Mary *smashes the other saucer.*

Sadie *screams.*

Standoff.

Simeon   Get out. Get out, get out! For God's sake, leave me alone.

Exit **Sadie** *and* **Mary**.

Simeon *surveys the broken crockery and torn up pamphlet.*

Simeon   What a bloody mess. Playing the tuba – who am I kidding? There's no way out for us; no way of crossing the breadline into a life worth living. We're trapped. Surviving, no more than that. What's it all amount to in the end, anyway, eh? (*He takes a gun out and places it on the table.*) The best anyone can hope for is someone there at the last, to chuck a few daffs on their grave. We're not bones and muscle, or even belly buttons. We're ashes and dust. (*Picks up the note he cast aside.*) – 'in the event of my death . . .' that'll do. (*Places note carefully on the table. Picks up gun and brings it up to his temple.*) Right Simeon Duff. Time to make egg flip. (*Screws up his face . . .*)

Victor (*off*)   Hello?

Simeon (*hides gun behind his back*)   Who's there?

Enter **Victor Stark**.

Victor   I'm so sorry.

Simeon   What are you sorry for?

Victor   I'm interrupting you?

Simeon   Nothing important.

Victor   I'm looking for a man called Duff.

Simeon   Simeon Duff? That's me. I am he.

Victor   How are you?

Simeon   I'm very well, thank you.

Victor   Oh.

He turns to leave.

Simeon   Where you going?

Victor   I don't think you're the man I'm looking for.

Simeon   I'm Simeon Duff.

Victor   And you're very well.

Simeon   I am.

Victor   Quite so. Sorry to have bothered you.

Simeon   What do you want with Simeon Duff?

Victor   Forgive me – the Simeon Duff I am looking for is planning to shoot himself.

Simeon   Who told you?

Victor   Are you?

Simeon   No. To shoot myself I'd have to have a gun and I haven't got a licence so . . .

Victor   So?

Simeon   I'm not him.

Victor *moves further into the room, and closer to the table.*

Victor   I have the correct address . . .

Simeon   How long do you get for illegal possession of a firearm?

Victor (*seeing the note*)   'In the event of my death, I blame no one.'

Simeon   Six months?

Victor   No one's going to arrest you, Simeon. How can they – if you're dead?

Simeon   What?

Victor   But this isn't the way.

Simeon   Don't try and stop me.

Victor   Do I look like a Samaritan?

Simeon   Eh?

Victor   'I blame no one?' Really? Don't you think that's rather a waste? You're going to shoot yourself /

Simeon   Don't try and stop me.

Victor   I wouldn't dream of it. Really. Young man, in his prime, glowing with health, best years ahead of him – suddenly takes arms against a sea of troubles and. . . 'Pchw'. (*Puts two fingers to his temple and makes shooting sound.*)

It's fantastic, I tell you. Inspiring. But to blame no one . . . ? The death of a young man should be meaningful. Resonant, you know? Don't you ever look outwards, Simeon, at the country? Poor healthcare, bad housing, substandard education, unemployment, low culture – the parlous state of our society – and yet the finest minds of our time are not heeded; summarily ignored by political masters, public institutions and common people. We might as well be silent. But a dead man, Simeon . . . is never silent. A dead man is loud. A dead man is eloquent. The only voice that can ever really be heard is a dead voice. You are a dead man, Duff – and so I come to you on behalf of the intellectual elite of our country to urge you to die – as a social activist.

Simeon   Come again?

Victor   Living is intolerable. Of course it is. But don't you see? Someone must be to blame for that. You are in despair, Duff. So tell me – whom do you accuse?

Simeon   Who do I . . . ?

Victor   Who's to blame?

Simeon   Theodore Hugo Shultz.

Victor   Ah . . . ?

Simeon   A cheat and a fraud. Should be locked up.

Victor   A banker! Yes. Of course. But don't accuse just him, Simeon. Finger the lot of 'em – the government, the media, the police . . . They're all guilty.

Simeon   They are?

Victor   I can see, Simeon, that you don't yet quite understand why you are shooting yourself. Perhaps I may offer some guidance . . . ?

Simeon   Please do.

Victor   You are making this ultimate sacrifice for the sake of Truth.

Simeon   I am?

Victor   But what is Truth?

Simeon   Don't know.

Victor   'Truth's a dog that must to kennel. He must be whipped out, when Lady Brach may stand by th' fire and stink.' Truth must be heard and quickly, powerfully! So tear up this note and write another. Name all those you accuse and demand that the world now pay attention to the formidable, compassionate socio-political writing of Victor Stark.

Simeon   Who?

Victor   Me. And once you have penned this eloquent indictment, Simeon, your self-destruction will no longer be the unremarkable demise of a pitiful nonentity. Your death will be a grand gesture – the clarion call that awakes the nation to a brave new world of social cohesion and justice. You'll be in the all the papers . . .

Simeon   On the telly?

Victor   Crowds will flock to line the streets in respectful silence as your funeral cortege passes by, a sleek black limousine; your coffin of stout English oak bedecked with summer blooms . . .

Simeon   A limo?

Victor   Your expiration will strike a clangorous chord with the collective social conscience. Your grave will become a place of pilgrimage for all those who wish to honour a true hero of the people. On this very boarding house I see . . . a blue plaque!

Simeon   Now that's living.

Victor   I envy you, Simeon. I really do. I'd shoot myself, but I must remain here a while longer, humbly to lead what will inevitably follow your noble sacrifice. (*Checks his watch.*) So – here's the plan. You rewrite your note, and . . . or perhaps I could draft something for you . . . ?

Simeon   No, I'll write it myself.

Victor   May I embrace you, Simeon Duff? You know . . . I didn't weep when my mother died. My dearest mother – but now . . . oh . . . oh . . . Anon.

Exit **Victor** *– deeply moved.*

Simeon   Did I . . . ? Did I just get a job? I did. At last – a purpose in life. Everything I've suffered finally makes sense. I will die for a higher ideal, and my name will be remembered forever. Victor Stark is right – they're all to blame, and I'll make 'em sorry they ever left Simeon Duff on the scrap heap. Oh yes . . . Where's the paper? What? There's no bloody paper left. Here am I about to make history and I've got nothing to write on. Mary!

Enter **Mary**.

Mary   I'm here, Simeon. Are you all right? Can I get you anything?

Simeon I'm going out. I need money.

Mary How much money?

Simeon Enough for some writing paper.

Mary I've got a jotter. You can have some of that.

Simeon Mary, I'm writing the Truth. This is a job for Basildon Bond.

Mary Oh well, in that case . . . I saved a bit on the offers this week.

She retrieves a few coins from a purse by the bed.

Simeon And while I'm out, scrub up, Mary, eh? Things are going to be different round here. You are the widow of an important figure in our country's history.

Mary What do you mean, Simeon?

Simeon I mean tidy yourself up, wash your hair, dab o' scent. You are a Duff Mary – and that means something.

Mary Oh Simeon, I'm so pleased you're being more positive about everything.

*Mary kisses **Simeon**. He responds . . .*

*Enter **Sadie**.*

Sadie There's a young woman downstairs asking for 'Monsieur' Simeon Duff. I reckon she's some brand of theatrical. Says it's a matter of life and death. I'll tell her you're busy.

Simeon I'll decide when I'm busy, Mother. Important people will be calling here more often now – get used to it. Show her up.

*Exit **Sadie** and **Mary**.*

Simeon *licks his hand and slicks back his hair.*

Simeon It's already started. And I'm not even dead yet.

Enter **Chloe MacSween**.

Chloe   Monsieur Duff?

Simeon   Oui, oui. I am he. The very same. In person.

Chloe   Make my acquaintance.

She holds out her hand for him to kiss.

I am Chloe MacSween, but you can call me Ma'm'selle.

Simeon   Mais oui – Ma'm'selle.

Chloe   I have something to ask, Monsieur. A petit favour.

Simeon   Happy to help, Ma'm'selle Chloe.

Chloe   Do it for me.

Simeon   Do what?

Chloe   Shoot yourself for me.

Simeon   I can't do that.

Chloe   Pourquoi?

Simeon   Poor who?

Chloe   Poor Simeon – who has shot himself for the love of a beautiful, unobtainable woman.

Simeon   Sorry, Ma'm'selle Chloe. I'm spoken for. I've already agreed to do it for someone else.

Chloe   Rosie Philpot! The scheming cow. She wants my Eddie.

Simeon   Your what?

Chloe   My Eddie. Eddie Parker. The love of my life. But if you shoot yourself for Rosie, he'll give himself to her instead. How did she manage to get to you before I did? Don't swallow it, Simeon. She's common fare – a hamburger, but I am pâté de foie gras. Pink champagne to her hand-pulled bitter.

Simeon   I like a pint.

Chloe   To her love is nothing more than lecherous groping and grunting and gratification of the flesh!

Simeon   Flesh?

Chloe   Flesh! But we are not animals, Monsieur. We are divine. Eddie is divine. He fills my soul.

Simeon   Soul?

Chloe   Soul. He's aloof, intense, mysterious, but a powerful, romantic gesture such as yours would reach him, touch him, move him. Shoot yourself for my sake, Monsieur Duff, and Eddie Parker would finally open his big brown eyes and notice me.

Simeon   I'd really like to help – but . . .

Chloe   Reject Rosie Philpot.

Simeon   I've never even met Rosie Philpot.

Chloe   Oh – you will. She'll be round before too long, in her tight crop tops. She'll tell you that her belly arouses men's passions. It's disgusting. I mean, it wasn't Helen's belly that launched a thousand ships, was it?

Simeon   I've never met Helen either.

Chloe   Look at me. What do you see? A face, Monsieur. The face that drove you to it. And if you come to my flat I'll show you my portfolio.

Simeon   !

Chloe   I have been photographed many times. My visage will inspire you to write your poetic, heartbreaking farewell note – telling how a cold, distant goddess drove you mad with unrequited passion. 'Oh, I would give my heart to death / To keep my honour fair; / Yet, I'll not give my inward faith / My honour's name to spare!' I know you feel this, Simeon. You are a man of deep, romantic sensibilities.

Simeon   It's true. I have always been a bit that way.

Chloe   Then come with me.

Sadie *pops her head in.*

Sadie   Kettle's on – will you have a cuppa tea, missus?

Simeon   We're going out, erm . . . woman. Would you mind just having a quick tidy round. There seems to have been an accident with some crockery here.

Sadie   You don't say!

Sadie *exits, muttering.*

Simeon   After you, Ma'm'selle.

Chloe   Merci, Monsieur.

Exit **Simeon** *and* **Chloe**.

Sadie *returns with dustpan and brush.*

Sadie   What a mess. I haven't seen such a heap of broken pots since the last tea dance at the Saint Vitus community centre.

She starts to sweep up.

Enter **Mary** *with towels and washbag.*

Sadie   Are you taking a bath, Mary Duff? It's not Sunday, is it?

Mary   Simeon told me to wash my hair and tidy myself up. I thought it might help.

Sadie   I reckon it's all blown over now.

Mary   I can't help worrying, Mam. Look at me – I'm a bag o' nerves.

Sadie   Have a sing in the shower and you'll feel all better again.

Exit **Mary**.

Sadie   Oh, but this was good china. Those Duffs are both off their feckin' heads, for sure – smashing up such lovely crock. Lord, and doesn't it go everywhere . . .

She gets down on all fours and reaches under the bed with the broom.

Enter **George Timms**, *with carrying a letter pad.*

Mary's *voice rises in song from the direction of the bathroom –* **A Bunch of Thyme**.

George *looks around, but doesn't see* **Sadie**, *who is half under the bed now.*

He creeps over to the bathroom door and peeps in.

Sadie   Well now, George Timms, what sort of pornography is this?

George   Mrs O'Toole! I didn't see you there.

Sadie   Obviously not, or you wouldn't have your winky-eye at the bathroom keyhole where there's a woman washing herself and most probably in the nip.

George   I wasn't peeping.

Sadie   Oh no?

George   I was looking at her from a Marxist point of view.

Sadie   And a bare-naked behind looks different from that point of view, does it?

George   Certainly. I've personally tested the theory many times.

You know on the first day of spring, when women have put their light summer clothes on for the first time while they're still carrying a little extra weight from the winter, and everything's just a bit too tight? A man could be driven wild with desire by all those curves and bulges – like a bowl of exotic fruit. But when I see one of those women coming towards me in the street I say to myself, 'George Timms, you will not objectify this comrade – you will look at her from a

Marxist point of view.' So I do – and in a flash the fruit is faded, and the woman goes from luscious peach to raw turnip – just like that. Nothing excites me now. I look at everything from a Marxist point of view. Do you want me to look at you like that?

Sadie   I most certainly do not!

George   Too late.

Sadie   Stop!

George   I'm doing it.

Sadie   Stop!

George   I'm doing it now.

Sadie   Help!

Mary *comes running on.*

Mary   What's up?

Sadie   What's up?

Mary   Someone's shouting.

Sadie   It's me.

Mary   You?

Sadie   George Timms has a point of view.

George   A Marxist point of view.

Sadie   He says it makes fat women look like turnips.

Mary   Are you wanting the loo, George? Bathroom's free now.

George   I don't need the toilet. I'm having trouble with punctuation.

Sadie   Me too. What do you take for it?

George   Do you know anything about the colon?

Sadie   A teaspoon of syrup o' figs usually fixes me.

George   I don't think mine's in the right place.

Sadie   You'll have to see a doctor about that, George.

George   I don't need a doctor to help with my writing.

Mary   You've been writing?

Sadie   That'll be why you're bunged up, George. You're in love!

George   In love?

Sadie   I hate to be the one to break it to you, George, but for a young feller you're a right auld stick-in-the-mud. So, if you've suddenly started expressing yourself in writing . . . well – a body doesn't have to be a psychotic to work that one out. You're obsessed.

George   I admit it. I am obsessed.

Sadie   And who is she? What's her name?

George   Al Bush.

Sadie   Holy Saint Hubert – I didn't see that one coming.

George   Man and boy, all I ever wanted to be was a postman. To deliver letters. But from the moment I set eyes on our landlord my peace was shattered – and I find I am compelled by a secondary urge – to *write* letters.

Mary   What is it about him, George?

George   His libido. His insatiable erotic appetite. His sexual energy. I've written this letter to the newspaper – only I think I need a colon. I'll read it to you, shall I?

Mary   If you think it would help.

George   Dear Ed – that's not his name, of course; it's short for Editor . . . I don't know his actual name. Dear Ed, scientists tell us that spots on the sun may be responsible for disturbances and trouble here on earth. Well – let me tell you that there is a spot much closer to home, responsible for equally unsettling effects on our own community. Alexander Peter Bush – live-in landlord and proprietor of the OK Corral Shooting Gallery at the Silver Nugget Amusement Arcade is a sexual sore on the face of our fair city.

We postal workers want to shoot, but the OK Corral is never open because Al Bush spends his whole time looking at women – from an un-Marxist point of view. At the moment it's Mrs Margaret Johnson, landlady of the Blind Piper public house. And if he isn't there, leering at her over the bar, he's entertaining her back at his boarding house.

Sadie   And him a grieving widow and all.

George   Al Bush's libido is infringing on the rights of postal workers to engage in the pleasant pastime of rifle target practice . . . a practice that may prove critical, come the Revolution. I urge the editor to expose Al Bush's wayward womanising and demand the immediate reopening of the Shooting Gallery. Yours sincerely, Thirty-five Thousand Postmen.

Sadie   How many?

Mary   You got thirty-five thousand people to sign your letter?

George   No. Just me. 'Thirty-five Thousand Postmen' is my nom de plume.

Sadie   God help him, he's gone up the yarn and round the twist.

George   I've got the envelope stamped and ready to go. I'm just not sure if I need a colon here . . . (*Shows letter to* **Mary**.)

Enter **Al** *and* **Maggie**.

Al   Is you're husband about, Mary?

Mary (*sotto*)   Al – you need to have a word with George.

Al   What's up, George?

George   Punctuation. (*Reads.*) '. . . to engage in the pleasant pastime of rifle target practice . . . a practice that may prove critical, come the Revolution . . .' Would you put a colon, between 'practice' and 'a practice'?

Al   Personally, I'd probably use a hyphen.

George   A hyphen! Why didn't I think of that? Far less bourgeois. (*He adds the hyphen to his letter.*) Thanks Al.

Al   Don't mention it.

Exit **George**.

Mary   Al! That was a letter of complaint about you.

Al   About me?

Sadie   And all your horny-porny hanky-panky.

Maggie   What trout have you been tickling this time, Al Bush?

Al   You're the only fish in my pond, Maggie.

Sadie   Yes it was you, Maggie. You're the trout.

Mary   It's a letter to the newspaper about you.

Maggie   And me?

Sadie   Slander and defecation.

Al   Why didn't you say so?

Mary   He's gone to post it now.

Al   Flamin' Nora.

Maggie   Stop him, Al!

Enter **Victor**.

Victor   Al – if I might have a word?

Al   Not now, Victor.

Exit **Al** *and* **Maggie**, *followed by* **Sadie** *and* **Mary**.

Enter **Nicholas Pugh** *(Welsh) – business suit over a butcher's apron.*

Pugh   Hello? Mr Duff, I presume? Mr Simeon Duff?

Victor   Good God, no.

Pugh   Do you know him?

Victor   I'm sorry – and you are . . . ?

Pugh   The name's Pugh. Nicholas Pugh. (*Hands over a business card.*) Pork and Leek a speciality.

Enter **Father MacLeod** *(Scots).*

MacLeod   Beg pardon – is either of you gentlemen a Mr Simeon Duff?

Pugh   He's not here.

MacLeod   Do you know where I might find him?

Victor   Has Mr Duff asked to see you, Father . . . ?

MacLeod   MacLeod.

Pugh   Pugh.

MacLeod   Pugh.

Pugh   MacLeod. (*Hands over a card.*) Pork and Leek a speciality.

Enter **Rosie Philpot**.

Rosie   Where is he?

Victor   Duff? Pugh? MacLeod?

Rosie   Bush!

Enter **Al** *– tearing up* **George**'s *letter, followed by* **Maggie**, *carrying her shoes.*

Pugh   Mr Bush.

Victor   Alexander.

Rosie   Al.

MacLeod   Sandy!

Al   Give me a minute, will you.

All   Where's Duff?

Rosie   Where's my money?

Al   Rosie.

Rosie   I want it back.

Al   Not now, Rosie.

Rosie   I saw Chloe MacSween in the arcade this morning.
She says Simeon Duff is shooting himself for her. What do
you take me for, eh? Think I wouldn't find out? You
promised him to me. I paid a deposit.

Al   Non-refundable.

Rosie   I haven't busted my overdraft limit so that Emily
bloody Brontë can have him.

Pugh   What about my down-payment, Bush? You told me I
was guaranteed.

Victor   Duff is mine. I've already spoken to him.

MacLeod   Good Lord – this is a man's life we are talking
about. A human life: precious, priceless and cannot
be bought.

Al   But in-so-far as that's possible, Father, your fifty quid
has also gone in the book.

Victor   You're all wasting your time. Mr Duff has already
chosen his cause célèbre – the intellectual life of our country,
led by the inspirational political writer, Victor Stark.

All   Who?

Victor   Me.

Al   Victor – I told you all communications with Simeon were to go through me. You had no right to /

Victor   Let your clients here find another corpse, Al. There'll be one along shortly, I'm sure.

Pugh   And how much longer do you think people like me can wait for the economy to get going? I'm having to let more staff go every week.

MacLeod   The greatest threat we face is spiritual bankruptcy.

Rosie   Political, economic, spiritual – all disasters made by men.

Maggie   She's got a point.

Rosie   Not real men though. Heavy breathers. Self-serving patriarchal tossers. What they need is sexual release – and until they get some /

Victor   If our leaders would only listen to Victor Stark /

Pugh   Who keeps this country working?

MacLeod   We must capture the hearts of the youth.

Victor   You're right about that, Father. Once upon a time, people had an ideal they were prepared to die for – and with that, they inspired others. Nowadays the people who want to die don't have any ideals, and the people with ideals don't want to die. Truth is – now, more than ever, we need dead ideologists.

Rosie   I'll tell you what I need – a living, breathing, red-blooded man. I need Eddie Parker. Big, beautiful, brown-eyed Eddie – best looking bloke on campus – but he's such a moody bugger. He's got to snap out of it. That's why I need Simeon Duff. If he kills himself for my sake, Eddie will love me.

Victor   Why would he do that?

Rosie   Because it's just the sort of thing to impress him – a man driven to extremities by naked desire.

Victor   He sounds like a very interesting young man.

Rosie   You're not kidding. He's got buns like beef tomatoes.

Pugh   We can't let the death of Duff be thrown away on a couple of randy undergraduates. It has to be a desperate cry for business and jobs.

MacLeod   A martyr for our Holy Mother, The Church.

Victor   A sign to reinvigorate political discourse.

Al   A lottery, friends – a lottery.

MacLeod   A what?

Al   A raffle, then.

Victor   A raffle?

Al   A sweep.

MacLeod   This is a human being, Sandy– not a tombola!

Al   You're quite right, Father. It would be immoral to sell this man's life to the highest bidder. But, given that he has reached this decision and will not be deflected from his course, it'd be a crying shame to let him go to waste.

Victor   I, for one, am not interested in sponsoring any man's death.

The death isn't important. It's what comes after that matters.

Maggie   You mean the wake?

Victor   I mean the worm. The worm that eats away – not at the corpse, but at the hearts of others, moved by a noble sacrifice: 'O rose, thou art sick /'

Rosie   No I'm not.

Victor   A chain reaction. I know a lot of young people – students – idealistic dreamers – like your Freddie –

Rosie   Eddie.

Victor   – frustrated, fierce . . . fragile. Young people, unspoiled, quixotic, in need of a noble cause. And if the worm were to get into one of them . . .

Enter **Simeon**.

Simeon   What's this? A party?

Victor   Word has got round about your grand gesture, and everyone wants to offer their support.

Simeon   My what?

Pugh   You're a hero.

MacLeod   A sacrificial lamb.

Rosie   A real man.

Simeon   Are you Rosie Philpot?

Victor   Have you decided when you'll do it?

Simeon   Do it? Oh. Dunno yet.

Rosie (*impressed*)   He's so casual.

Victor   How about twelve noon tomorrow?

Simeon   Tomorrow?

Victor   If you can wait that long /

Pugh   A bit of a do –

Maggie   At the Blind Piper.

Al   Champagne breakfast.

MacLeod   Final blessing.

Maggie   I'll do you a good deal.

Victor   Ten o'clock suit you?

Maggie   That'd be fine.

Victor   Ten o'clock, everyone?

All   Fine / grand / I'm free.

Al   Ten o'clock Simeon.

Simeon   Ten o'clock.

Pugh   I'll provide sausages.

Simeon   Sausages?

Pugh   Pork and Leek a speciality.

Victor   Send you on your way.

Simeon   On my way to where?

Victor   Ah! Wouldn't we all like to know the answer to that.

MacLeod   We certainly would.

Rosie   We'll pick you up.

Victor   Tomorrow at ten, Simeon. Tomorrow at ten.

All exit except **Simeon**.

Simeon   Tomorrow. Tomorrow. Tomorrow.

I guess we've all gotta go sometime. If I didn't die yesterday, and I don't die today, I'll surely die tomorrow. Blimey – I feel as old as the universe – from end to end. All of time . . . time . . . What does that mean?

You hold a gun to your head and time passes, a second – a tick of the clock – and another – tock. But between the tick and the tock there's this void to cross. A quantum leap has to be made between the tick and the tock and if you don't make it . . . Tick – a man is a man. Tock – a man is no more. Nothing.

And the trigger of the gun – that's the key isn't it: the key that opens the void. You flick the safety catch – click. You squeeze the trigger – bang! Click – a man is a man. Bang – a man is no more.

Now – I've got a fair idea about the tick and the click . . . but the tock and the bang? 'Tick and click' is here, now, lodgings, wife, mother-in-law, ten fingers, ten toes, sun, sky, scrap heap. But what's 'tock and bang', eh? It's none of those things, and I can't imagine that . . . no lodgings, no wife, no mother-in-law (well, maybe I could stretch to imagining that) but you get my drift. Nothing. No Simeon Duff.

And what's Simeon Duff anyway? A man. What is a man? A piece of work? A temple of the soul – is that it? And when the temple is torn down what happens to the soul? Does it fly around like a burst balloon? And is it glad to be free of all the suffering in the world? Are the pearly gates shining? Does Saint Peter see you and say, 'come on, lad, your troubles are over – from now on it's egg flip all the way'? Will I fall asleep in the arms of Jesus? Or is it all – just – nothing . . .

Three **Gypsies** *enter – carrying clocks.*

And is nothing any worse than this?

The clocks chime the hour.

Tomorrow it is. Tomorrow, at noon.

Gypsies (*sing*)   No more picking at navel fluff
  Problem solved with a pinch of snuff
  He said he'd do it – they called his bluff
  O Simeon, Simeon Duff
  O Simeon, Simeon . . . Duff.

Interval.

Act Three

The next day, at the Blind Piper public house.

A bar; tables; chairs; a sign for the GENTS toilet.

A **Gypsy trio** *of musicians.*

Al, **Victor**, **MacLeod**, **Pugh**, **Rosie**, **Chloe** *all seated round pub tables.*

Simeon *also seated, covered in party popper streamers.*

Everyone is worse for drink – especially **Father MacLeod**.

Music.

Gypsies (*sing*) **Cardinal Puff (Original)**

> He's one of the lads, he's giving it large,
> He's really knocking it back.
> He's making merry, he's taking charge,
> He's always up for the craic.

> He's our Simeon, your Simeon,
> Everyone's Simeon Duff.
> Generous host,
> Drinking a toast to, Cardinal Puff!

Simeon I drink a toast to Cardinal Puff for the first time today.

Taps forefinger of right hand on table x 1.
Taps forefinger of left hand on table x 1.
Taps forefinger of right hand under table x 1.
Taps forefinger of left hand under table x 1.
Snaps fingers of right hand x 1.
Snaps fingers of left hand x 1.
Picks up beer with forefingers and thumbs – and drinks.

Gypsies And . . . drink, drink, drink, drink.

All Drink, drink, drink!

Cheer!

Pugh   What a man!

Chloe   Darcy, Rochester, Heathcliffe . . .

Rosie   Duff!

MacLeod   God bless him.

Enter **Maggie** *with a crate of beers.*

Maggie   Here's another crate. I've put in on the slate.

Al   Keep it coming, Maggie love. Keep it coming.

Simeon   Maggie – what time is it?

Maggie   What do you want to know that for, Simeon? It's way off noon, if that's what you're asking.

Simeon   Is it?

Maggie   You've ages yet.

Simeon   But I think /

Maggie   Don't think. Drink!

She hands him another bottle and pushes him back in his seat.

MacLeod (*to* **Chloe**)   You like literature, my dear?

Chloe   It's my passion.

MacLeod   May I recite some Robert Burns?

Chloe   My love is like a red red rose?

MacLeod   Aye – something like that.

Simeon   Al, what time is it?

Al *is laughing with* **Victor**.

MacLeod   There was twa wifes, an twa witty wifes,
  As e'er played houghmagandie,
  An they cuist oot, upon a time,
  Oot ower a drink o brandy;

Simeon   Ms Philpot? Rosie!

Rosie (*to* **Chloe**)   I've heard this poem – it's filthy.

MacLeod   Up Maggy rose, an forth she gaes,
An she leaves auld Mary flytin,
An she farted by the byre-en'
For she was gaun a-shitin.

Chloe   Stop it. Stop it now! I don't like smut.

MacLeod   Pity.

Simeon   Mr Pugh.

Pugh   Nicholas.

Simeon   Nicholas. What time is it?

MacLeod   Is there a problem, Simeon?

Simeon   I think so.

MacLeod   You know if a man has a problem there can only be one of two reasons. Either he isn't praying enough, or he isn't drinking enough.

Simeon   But I think / (it might be time)

Maggie   Don't think. Drink!

Gypsies (*sing*)   He's our Simeon, your Simeon,
Everyone's Simeon Duff.
Generous host,
Drinking a toast, to Cardinal Puff!

Simeon   I drink a toast to Cardinal Puff Puff for the second time today.

Taps two fingers of right hand on table x 2.
Taps two fingers of left hand on table x 2.
Taps two fingers of right hand under table x 2.
Taps two fingers of left hand under table x 2.
Snaps fingers of right hand x 2.
Snaps fingers of left hand x 2.

Picks up beer with two fingers and thumbs – and drinks.

Gypsies   And . . . drink, drink, drink, drink.

All   Drink, drink, drink!

Cheer!

Victor *rises to his feet, tinkle of glass for attention.*

Victor   Thank you, friends. Your attention, please.

Bit of shushing and murmurs of 'ooh, speech!' etc . . .

Victor   I feel that someone ought to say a few words on this unique occasion. And as we have the compassionate and insightful political writer Victor Stark in our midst, it seems fitting that he should speak on behalf of everyone.

Victor *sits.*

A beat.

Victor *stands.*

Victor   Dear friends – how often can we say that we are witnessing a fellow human being rise to greatness and glory? For that is surely where our friend Simeon Duff is bound.

All   Hear, hear (*etc . . .*)

Simeon   Is it time?

Chloe   We need a poem about roses.

MacLeod   Roseberry to his lady says,
  'My hinnie an my succour,'
  O shall we dae the thing you ken,
  'Or shall we tak oor supper?'

Victor   Father MacLeod /

MacLeod   Wi modest face, sae fou o grace,
  Replied the bonny lady;
  'My noble lord dae as you please,
  But supper is na ready.'

Maggie   Will you have another drink, Father?

MacLeod   Don't mind if I do.

Victor   With his grand gesture, Simeon Duff has already brought together, in this very room, old and young; male, female; believer and atheist; the uneducated and the towering intellect. And we can only imagine the force and power of this courageous act. . . afterwards. Therefore I invite you to stand and raise your glass to a man exundating with intrinsic exuperance. A toast – to the bodacious, parabolical intrepidity of your own, your very own, Simeon Duff!

All   Simeon Duff.

Chloe   My heart is breaking.

Pugh   My stomach's churning.

Victor   I didn't cry when my own mother died, but . . .

Al   Would you like to say anything, Simeon?

Simeon   What time is it?

Maggie   Never mind that. Drink!

All   Drink!

Gypsies (*sing*)   He's our Simeon, your Simeon,
Everyone's Simeon Duff.
Generous host,
Drinking a toast, to Cardinal Puff!

Simeon   I drink a toast to Cardinal Puff Puff Puff for the third time today.

Taps three fingers of right hand on table x 3.
Taps three fingers of left hand on table x 3.
Taps three fingers of right hand under table x 3.
Taps three fingers of left hand under table x 3.
Snaps fingers of right hand x 3.
Snaps fingers of left hand x 3.

Picks up beer with three fingers and thumbs – and drinks.

Gypsies　And . . . drink, drink, drink, drink.

All　Drink, drink, drink!

Gypsies (*sing*)　He's one of the lads, he's giving it large,
He's really knocking it back.
He's making merry, he's taking charge,
He's always up for the craic.
So –
Drain the bottle, and drain the barrel.
Yes drain it, every drop.

MacLeod　Once a Cardinal, always a Cardinal!

All　Drink and never stop!

Cheer!

Simeon *tips the bottle over his head and staggers back into his seat.*

Pugh　I'm all wound up, I am. We must sing something
sweeter. Simple and soothing for the shipment of the soul.
You look at me and what do you see? A butcher, a
businessman, a brute – but I have music in my heart, and a
tender heart it is too. When I butcher a carcass, I do it with
love – real love. (*He pulls a wad of cash from his pocket and tips
the musicians.*) Play my favourite.

Gypsies (*play*)　**Fiddlers' Green (By John Conolly)**

Pugh (*sings*)　As I roved by the dockside one evening so
rare
To view the still waters and take the salt air
I spied an old fisherman singing a song
Oh, take me away boys me time is not long

Pugh *weeps.* **Victor** *passes him a tissue.*

All　Dress me up in mi oilskins and jumpers
No more on the docks I'll be seen
Just tell me old shipmates, I'm taking a trip mates
And I'll see you someday in Fiddlers' Green

MacLeod   Now Fiddlers' Green is a place I've heard tell
Where the fishermen go if they don't go to hell

Al   And the girls are all pretty and the beer is all free
And there's bottles of rum growing on every tree

All   Dress me up in mi oilskins and jumpers
No more on the docks I'll be seen
Just tell me old shipmates, I'm taking a trip mates
And I'll see you someday in Fiddlers' Green

Victor   Why are you weeping, Nicholas?

Pugh   I'm weeping for my homeland – my long lost homeland.

Victor   Why, where you from?

Pugh   Prestatyn.

Victor   You're right, Nicholas, to mourn – for not only have we lost our homeland, but she has lost us. (*Rises to his feet.*) O how I would love to glide at high speed by the golden fields of Albion aboard the driver's cab of a class 390 Pendolino. To hear the strings of the Celtic harp burst and the engine driver weeping in his peaked cap. My homeland – whose fertile earth is nourished by the bones of countless poets: Burns and Thomas, Yeats and Shakespeare. O to ride the island rail from highland peak, by rocky shore, to verdant Wiltshire wold, where I might hurl myself into a haystack and pray, swear, blaspheme, repent and quench my craw with a flagon of foaming English ale. And in my grief my soul should tear itself from my flesh and take flight – over the landscape carved by the sword of Arthur Pendragon, Robin of Loxley and Sigurd the Stout – and I would fly, fly, fly like an arrow over the fells and dells, faster and faster – and o, my soul! O my country! If you could only speak, what would you say to me?

Enter **George** *from the GENTS.*

George   Bathroom's free . . .

Pugh *gets to his feet.*

George   Might want to . . . give it a minute . . .

Simeon   George. I didn't know you were coming.

George   I'm looking for Al. He gave me his word yesterday that he would open the shooting gallery this morning. I've done my round, and now I'm after a spot of target practice.

Maggie   George. Why don't you join us?

George   I don't drink.

MacLeod   What did he say?

Chloe   He doesn't drink, Father?

MacLeod   What's wrong with him?

George   There'll be no drinking after the Revolution.

Maggie   How about for the ladies.

George   Come the Revolution, there'll be no ladies either.

MacLeod   There was twa wifes /

Maggie   That'll do, Father.

Pugh   But without ladies, humanity would die out.

George   Come the Revolution there'll be no humans either. Just the masses.

MacLeod   Masses?

Pugh   Masses of masses.

MacLeod   You'll be needing priests then.

Al   Drink to the masses, George.

George   That puts me in a very difficult position. I don't drink, but I cannot refuse to drink to the masses.

Al   Maggie.

Maggie *hands* **George** *a drink.*

Al   A toast.

MacLeod   The ladies.

Pugh   The humans.

George   The masses.

MacLeod   Amen.

All drink.

Pugh   Let's have another song.

Simeon   I didn't care much for that last one.

Pugh   That was my favourite. It's about heaven.

Simeon   Is there life after death?

George   I don't want songs about heaven. I want to hear songs about the workers – and if there aren't any someone needs to write one.

Pugh   Victor's a writer.

Victor   I am something of a polymath. Renaissance man, if you will.

George   What do you write about?

Victor   Everything.

George   William Shakespeare was supposed to have written about everything, but he didn't write about postal workers, did he.

Victor   I wrote a poem about dockers.

George   Why would I want to read about dockers? I'm a postman.

Simeon   George – what about life after death?

Maggie   Never mind about that, Simeon. Drink.

Chloe   Bonjour, Monsieur George.

George   !

Chloe   I am Ma'm'selle MacSween. Make my acquaintance.

Holds out her hand for kissing.

George   I don't kiss.

Chloe   Pourquoi, Monsieur?

George   Are you from abroad?

Chloe   Non, Monsieur. But j'adore la France; et le gai Paris.

George   Paris.

Chloe   The most romantic city in the world.

George   I'd like to go there. They had a Revolution. And the first thing I'd do is find the Eiffel tower . . .

Chloe   Me too.

George   I'd climb right to the very top and look out over the river and rooftops of Paris – a good long look – from a Marxist point of view.

Chloe   I don't understand.

George   How could you? You're too bourgeois.

Victor   And when the Revolution comes, George – who do you think will make it happen?

George   The workers.

Victor   No – the bourgeoisie – for want of a better word.

George   How d'you work that out?

Victor   Perhaps I can explain it to you in the form of a parable . . . ? Once upon a time some duck eggs were placed beneath a good and faithful chicken. And that chicken sat brooding on the duck eggs for years, warming them with her body until finally, one day, they hatched out. But then the ducklings, in their excitement, grabbed the chicken and dragged her to the pond. 'Swim!' they cried. 'Swim, mother!'

Al   But the chicken'll drown.

Victor   That's because the chicken stands for the intellectual elite. We don't like getting our feet wet.

Al   Or your hands dirty.

Victor   The ducks are the proletariat – you, George. We have nurtured you, but when you finally emerge from your shell, you'll take charge and try to drown us.

George   Well if you can't swim, why don't you fly away?

Al   Chickens can't fly either.

George   So what do you do?

Victor   We don't 'do' anything. We sit.

George   You sit.

Victor   Yes. Sit.

George   Then the Revolution will never come.

Victor   Yes it will, because now we have Simeon Duff: an egg about to crack.

George   And what will you do, Simeon – when the eggs are cracked?

Simeon   Make egg flip.

Al   You'll be needing brandy for that. Brandy, Maggie!

MacLeod   My Maggie haes a mark,

Ye'll finnd it in the dark . . .

Simeon   Friends – seems to me you're all very clever and well read on politics and chickens and that – so maybe you can answer a question for me. Is there life after death?

Al   I think that's one for the Padre. What do you say, Father?

MacLeod   What's that?

Simeon   Is there life after death?

MacLeod   Ah . . . now . . . how would you like me to answer that? According to religion, or science, or Robbie Burns?

Simeon   Is there a difference?

MacLeod   Certainly. On the subject of life after death:religion says 'yes'; science says 'no'; and Robbie says 'there's no such uncertainty as a sure thing . . .'

Simeon   Meaning?

MacLeod   I'm buggered if I know. What are you asking me for anyhow? You'll find out for yourself in about half an hour.

Simeon   Half an hour? But I feel so alive. Is this when life begins? Half an hour before it's due to end?

Victor   Simeon – it's not for you to fret over the vagueries of eternal life. For you immortality is assured.

Simeon   That's right, Victor. Thank you for bringing me back to the point of it all. Alive, I'm nothing – a no-mark. But in death, I'll be famous. I'll speak out – my voice will be heard, crying out that I couldn't go on living because . . . because . . . what was it again, Victor? Why can't I go on?

Victor   Here's your note, Simeon. Your post mortem manifesto. I took the liberty of putting your inmost thoughts down on paper. Perhaps you'd like to copy it out.

Simeon   Thanks, Victor. I just need to know why – you know. Then I can get on with the job.

Victor *passes pen and paper to* **Simeon***, who begins copying.*

Pugh   All our causes are included in the note, aren't they, Victor?

Victor   Of course, Nicholas. Of course.

Chloe (*of* **Simeon**)   Look at him – like Abelard writing to Heloise.

MacLeod   They castrated him, you know.

Chloe   Who?

MacLeod   Abelard. (*Makes a scissor snip with his fingers.*)

Rosie   Every man seems smaller at the side of Simeon Duff. Even Eddie Parker. I saw him this morning and he looked pale and puny . . .

Victor   The worm is feeding already.

Al   Chicks, ducks, and now worms. Mind like a sodding zoo.

Pugh   I feel a bit sick, actually.

Chloe (*to* **MacLeod**)   There's a statue of Abelard at the Louvre.

Victor   I've seen it. You can't tell . . . (*that he's been castrated*).

Rosie   You've been to France?

Victor   Bien sûr.

Rosie   What size are French women's breasts?

Victor   I can't say I noticed.

Rosie   That's because in France it doesn't matter; a woman's breasts can be any size they want.

Pugh   Sick. Any minute now.

MacLeod   In sober oors I am a priest;
   A hero when I'm tipsey, O;
   But I'm a king an every thing,
   When wi a wanton Gipsey, O.

Simeon   Done. There it is – I have made my mark. When I was a kid I wanted to be a hero, but my parents were dead against it. Well, now look who's the man here now, eh? All you lot – you're afraid. I can see it in your eyes. None of you know the day, or the hour. But I do. I'm the only one not living in fear now. Up to this very moment I've been nothing more than a national insurance number, a statistic – the sum of boxes ticked on a social security form. Not any more. Life has brought me down, but I'm gonna take control and change that – and lift myself up out of the pit of obscurity to righteous . . . glorious . . .

Clock strikes twelve.

Simeon   I think that clock's fast.

George   I make it bang on.

Simeon   Bang on.

Maggie   Time to go, Simeon.

Victor   Time to go.

Pugh   Go well.

MacLeod   God bless.

Rosie   Goodbye.

Al   Good luck.

Chloe   Bon voyage.

George   Come and see us again soon.

Simeon   No, George, next time it's your turn to come to me.

All (*sing*)   Now I don't want a harp nor a halo, not me
   Just give me a breeze and a good rolling sea
   I'll play me old squeeze-box as we sail along
   With the wind in the riggin' to sing me a song

Simeon *exits, then returns and picks up a bottle and exits again.*

Maggie *starts to clear up;* **Al** *counts his money;* **Pugh** *vomits;*
Victor *weeps;* **Rosie** *and* **Chloe** *embrace in sisterly fashion;*
MacLeod *passes out;* **George** *carries on drinking, oblivious.*

   Dress me up in me oilskin and jumpers
   No more on the docks I'll be seen
   Just tell me old shipmates, I'm taking a trip mates
   And I'll see you someday in Fiddlers' Green

Act Four

An hour later.

The boarding house again; this time without the bedroom, but with the kitchen.

A table and chairs; odd sticks of kitchen furniture; window; doors.

Sadie *whisks up an egg flip at the table, on which lies the detritus from her efforts, and a jug of water.*

Sadie (*sings*) **A Bunch of Thyme (Traditional)**

> Come all ye maidens young and fair
> And you that are blooming in your prime
> Always beware and keep your garden fair
> Let no man steal away your thyme

Mary *joins in offstage.*

> For thyme it is a precious thing
> And thyme brings all things to my mind

Enter **Mary** *– with curlers.*

> Thyme with all its labours, along with all its joys
> Thyme, brings all things to my mind

Mary   What do you think, Mam? Big curls or little ones?

Sadie   What you curling for?

Mary   I want to look nice for Simeon when he comes in at dinnertime.

Sadie   You'd better get a wriggle on. It's almost one o'clock.

Mary   You made him an egg flip.

Sadie   It's a day of celebration. There's a cheese pie in the oven as well.

Mary   He didn't give you any sort of clue as to what we're celebrating?

Sadie   Just said that he'd got a job and he went out looking like the tit that got the top of the milk.

Mary   It was a job – and not just an interview?

Sadie   I reckon it's to do with all the fancy types and thespionics I've found myself making tea for lately.

Mary   He should have woken me before he left.

Sadie   You were all clapped out after that shenanigans the other night. Sure, he'll be full of it when he gets in.

Mary   Yes. So – big or little?

Sadie   ?

Mary   Curls.

Sadie   Big at the back, little round the front. Then he can look at you whichever way he likes best.

Mary   This is the turning point for us, Mam, isn't it? Things are going to get better from now on.

Sadie   Well, they couldn't get much worse.

Mary   What's this letter?

Sadie   What letter?

Mary   It's addressed to you.

Sadie   Is it? Well, I don't know, do I. I'm up to my eyes in pie and egg flip. Read it out.

Mary *opens and reads.*

Mary   'Dear Mother – by the time you read this I will be gone forever. Please break the news to Mary as gently as you can . . .'

Sadie   Holy Saint Hubert! (*Grabs the letter and reads.*) 'Send my good coat to our Billy – he could do with it – and put the rest of my stuff in the bin. I won't be needing anything any more. Goodnight and God bless . . .'

Mary   Oh. Oh God, Simeon. What have you done?

Sadie (*crossing herself, mumbling*)   Hail Holy Queen, mother of mercy. Hail our lives, our sweetness and our hope . . .

Enter **Victor**, **MacLeod**, **Al**, **Maggie**.

MacLeod   Mrs Duff? Morag.

Al   Mary.

MacLeod   Mary, my child. My prayers and condolences to you and your bairns. Your husband, the father of your little ones, is no more.

Al   He never was.

MacLeod   Never was what?

Al   The father of her little ones.

MacLeod   You mean someone else . . . ?

Al   I mean there are no little ones.

MacLeod   Oh, well that's one blessing, I suppose.

Al   Mary, I'm so sorry.

Victor   Your husband has made a grand gesture on behalf of the people of this country and the greater good. His renunciation will generate successive rings of reactionary ripples – like a pebble tossed in a pond. He may have perished, but his corpse is very much alive.

Mary   Where is he, I want to see him.

Victor   He is lying across the path of destiny . . .

Sadie   Is that the one down by the allotments?

Victor   The path of which I speak is allegorical – and all who travel that road will stumble over the body of Simeon Duff.

Al   He went down to the dockside to do it. Someone's gone there now to fetch him back.

Sadie   We'll have him here. I'll lay him out myself, like we did at home.

Mary   Oh, Simeon. Darlin', Sim.

Maggie   What are you going to wear for the funeral, Mary? You'll need something new. Something snazzy.

Sadie   Maggie Johnson, are you completely off your crate? We haven't enough money to bury the poor fecker, never mind forking out for widow's weeds.

Victor   Don't worry about money. It's all taken care of.

MacLeod   A solemn Requiem, with all the trimmings.

Al   Plot, headstone, coffin, catering – all taken care of.

Maggie   And a new outfit for you, Mary.

Victor   It will be a great occasion – with so many wishing to pay their respects. I have alerted the media . . .

Sadie   You mean the telly?

Victor   Simeon may be the first – but he won't be the last.

Al   Your husband died a hero, Mary.

Mary   What kind of hero?

Al   Political, religious, romantic, economic: right, left and centre – he'd pretty much covered all the bases.

MacLeod   A voice of grace, in this graceless age.

Maggie   You might want lace, but I think that's a bit flash, myself. Go for pleats. Or I suppose you could risk a little flare in the skirt.

Sadie   Can she have flared pleats?

Maggie   And a hat, of course.

Sadie   With a classy bit o' net stuck on the front.

Maggie   Here's a card for Kylie's Kloset.

Sadie That posh boutique!

Maggie Kylie's expecting you this afternoon. (*Hands card to* **Mary**, *who takes it automatically.*)

Victor Nothing but the best for the widow of Simeon Duff: Hero of Truth, whose lifeless eyes now light the way – looking ever in the direction of the profound political discourse of Victor Stark.

Sadie Who?

Victor Me. Permit me to kiss you on behalf of a grateful nation.

Victor *kisses* **Mary**.

Al And me too. The nation is very very grateful.

Maggie I think we should leave Mrs Duff to her prayers at this difficult time.

Maggie *drags* **Al** *away – exit.*

Victor In time, Mrs Duff, in time – like a pebble tossed into a pond.

MacLeod Come and see me, my dear – if you need to get anything off your chest.

Sadie Thank you, Father. We appreciate that, so we do.

Exit **Victor**, **MacLeod**.

Well, what fine people. What lovely people. Don't you think so, Mary? The world is full of kindness.

Mary The world is empty without Simeon.

Sadie What time is your fitting with the dressmaker?

Mary (*checks card*) Three o'clock.

Sadie 'Kylie's Kloset' – that'll be a dear do.

Mary I don't care.

Sadie   Do you think she'd do two for the price of one?

Mary   I don't care!

Sadie   Oh, but think of the hat.

Mary   So I'll have a hat – but no Simeon. This morning I had Simeon –

Sadie   – but no hat. Oh Lord – if only you could give us everything at once.

Enter two **Gypsies**, *carrying* **Simeon**'s *lifeless body – blood at his right temple.*

Mary   Simeon! Mother – oh Mother!

Sadie   Put him over here, on the table. I'll see to him, after that.

The **Gypsies** *dump* **Simeon** *on the kitchen table.*

Mary   Oh Sim. Darlin', Simeon!

Gypsy 1   We were just too late.

Gypsy 2   I'm sorry.

Sadie   Did you see what happened?

Gypsy 1   He shared his last drink with us.

Gypsy 2   He said, 'take me home'.

Gypsy 1   'Take me home,' he said.

Gypsy 2   We didn't know what he meant. And then he stepped behind the wall.

Gypsy 1   We thought he'd just gone for a . . . you know.

Gypsy 2   Thought nothing of it and then . . .

Gypsy 1   Bang!

Gypsy 2   A flock of seagulls lifted off the water . . .

Gypsy 1   Up they went –

Gypsy 2   And down he went –

Gypsy 1   Like a chimney-stack.

Gypsy 2   There was nothing we could have done.

Gypsy 1   'Take me home.'

Gypsy 2   'Take me home', he said.

Gypsy 1   So we did.

Mary *weeps.*

Gypsy 1   Very sorry, missus.

Gypsy 2   Very sorry indeed.

Sadie   Thanks for your trouble.

Exit **Gypsies** – **Sadie** *calling after.*

Would you like some egg flip? They've gone. Pity to waste it. (**Sadie** *drinks the egg flip while* **Mary** *continues to weep over* **Simeon**.) I'll fetch a bowl and wash him down now. Get him done before he stiffens up.

Mary   Oh Simeon. I tried. I tried to save you, I did everything I could. I don't understand. I thought things were changing for the better. Oh Sim, I can't believe you're dead.

Simeon   Dead? Dead? Who's dead?

Mary/Sadie   Ahhh!

Simeon   Oooooh – hold me. Hold on tight!

Mary   Simeon!

Sadie   Frightened the shite out of me, Lord Jesus.

Simeon   I'm flying. I'm with the angels.

Mary   Simeon, it's me – Mary.

Simeon   Mary? Mary, Mother of Jesus? Mary Madgalene? (*He touches the wound on his temple and sees the blood on his hand.*) Bloody Mary!

Mary   Simeon. It's me, Mary Duff.

Simeon   Mary Duff, are you dead too?

Mary   He's lost his mind, Mother.

Simeon   I'm the spirit of Simeon Duff.

Sadie   Spirit, b'Jesus! That's true enough – catch the whiff of him.

Mary   He's drunk!

Simeon (*to* **Sadie**)   Are you the Holy Mother?

Sadie   No, Simeon Duff, I am your *unholy* Mother-in-law! Jug Mary, get the jug.

Mary *picks up the jug from the table and, after a nod from* **Sadie**, *tips water over* **Simeon**.

Simeon   What did you do that for?

Mary   How could you, Simeon? How could you? You leave a note saying you're going to kill yourself, then people come and tell me you've done it, then more people come and bring you in, all limp and lifeless and covered in blood, and here am I, the inconsolable widow, weeping and wailing over your poor broken body and you're not even bloody dead!

Simeon   What time is it?

Sadie   About half one.

Simeon   Half past one? How did that happen? I was supposed to have . . . at twelve noon I was supposed to have . . . how did I get here? I was at the docks. We had a drink.

Sadie   You don't say.

Simeon   For courage. Dutch courage. I went behind the wall – and I thought I could do it, but I couldn't. I just couldn't bring myself to, you know – and I was dying for a wazz. I'd had a lot to drink. But as I was standing there, I had the gun in my hand like – I must have squeezed the trigger.

Mary   You must have passed out. You hit your head.

Sadie   It's a miracle he didn't shoot his auld feller clean off.

Simeon   Oh God, has anyone been here yet?

Sadie   The priest, Al Bush, Maggie Johnson – and some sackless gobshite of a poet.

Simeon   What did they say?

Sadie   He kept blathering on about pebbles.

Mary   They said they'd pay to bury you, and that you were a hero.

Sadie   Mary was getting a new hat.

Mary   We'll have to stop them, Mam – or we'll have to pay.

Sadie   Let's get over to Kylie's Kloset right away.

Simeon   No. Wait. There's time. I could still shoot myself.

Sadie   Oh for the love of Mike, will you leave it alone.

Simeon   I will. You'll see. I'll shoot myself.

Mary   You don't have it in you, Simeon.

Sadie   And anyways – you could shoot yourself right between the ears and still miss your brain by about three feet. So – while we're out, you can sober up, put the kettle on, and make a pot of tea. (*Mutters.*) Ya feckin' eejit!

Exit **Sadie** *and* **Mary**.

Simeon   Don't have it in me? I'll show them. I'll shoot myself right now, straight through the heart. Then they'll be sorry. (*Takes gun from his pocket.*) Got to do it quick though. Can't think about it for too long. (*Points gun at chest, moving it*

around, but realises that he doesn't know exactly where his heart is.)
Maybe not through the heart. In the mouth. That's quickest
of all. (*Puts gun in mouth. Takes it out again.*) I'll count to three.
(*Puts gun back in mouth.*) O . . . Oooo . . . Eeee (*Takes gun out.*)
No – I'll count to a thousand. (*Gun back in mouth.*) O . . .
Oooo . . . Eeee . . . Orrrr . . . Iiiii . . . (*He gags. Gun out.*) No,
if I'm going to count it'll have to be through the heart. (*Gun
to heart.*) And it's chicken counting to a thousand. I've got to
be more decisive. I'll count to a hundred and then it's
goodbye cruel world! No – better still, to fifteen. Here we go
– one, two three, four, five, six, seven, eight, nine, ten . . .
eleven . . . tweeellllvvvee . . . thiiiiiirrrrteeeeeeeeen . . .
fouuuuuurteeeeeen . . . Counting's rubbish. I'll never do it if
I count, I'll just do it straight away, in the mouth, no messin'.
(*Gun in mouth – and out again.*) Hang on though – if you do it
in the mouth it makes a right mess of your face, doesn't it.
(*Points to head.*) (*Points to heart.*) I can find my heart now, it's
beating that fast. In fact, I feel a bit faint. Oh, God I'm
palpitating – I'm having a heart attack. That's no bloody
good. If I die of a heart attack how the hell am I going to
shoot myself?

Enter **Undertakers 1** *and* **2**, *carrying a coffin – struggling.*

Undertaker 1   To me a bit.

Undertaker 2   To you.

Undertaker 1   Turn it slightly – or it'll not go through.

Undertaker 2   Careful now. To you.

Undertaker 1   Woaah!

Simeon *thrusts the gun back into his pocket.*

Simeon   Can I help you?

Undertaker 1   If you could just grab this end . . .

Simeon *helps them carry the coffin.*

Undertaker 2   On the table all right?

Simeon   Fine.

Undertaker 2   We were told to bring it here. We
understand that family members are preparing the body.

Simeon   Er, yes – the body is being prepared.

Undertaker 1   Very sorry for your loss, sir.

Simeon   Thank you.

Undertaker 1   I'll get the flowers.

Exit **Undertaker 1**.

Undertaker 2   Is the deceased not here?

Simeon   Yes. I mean, he's here in spirit . . . and I'm
expecting him to be here . . . in body – any time now.

Undertaker 2   Lovely casket, that. Top quality. He must
have been a very important man. I'm ashamed to say, I'd
never heard of him until now. Pity really, that people have to
die before you get to get to hear about them. Will it be open?
The casket? For viewing of the body.

Simeon   I don't think so.

Undertaker 2   Messy one, was it?

Simeon   In what sense? Oh, I see. Yes – I think you'd say
that it is all a terrible mess.

Undertaker 1 *returns with arms full of wreaths and flowers*.

Simeon   What's all that?

Undertaker 1   Tributes.

Undertaker 2   Condolences.

Undertaker 1   Eulogies.

Simeon (*reads a card*)   'Rest in peace, Simeon Duff – The
People's Prince.'

Undertaker 2 The dockside, where the deceased . . . deceased, is already filling up with flowers, tokens, balloons . . .

Undertaker 1 Teddies . . .

Simeon (*reads another card*) 'You will live on in our hearts – Goodnight sweet prince.'

Undertaker 1 They're holding a candlelit vigil tonight.

Undertaker 2 Ostentatious and devoted obsequies.

Undertaker 1 It's going to be a massive funeral.

Undertaker 2 Which must be a consolation to you.

Simeon Not really.

Undertaker 1 Our condolences.

Undertaker 2 Our sincere condolences.

Simeon Me too.

Exit **Undertakers**.

Simeon *takes the gun out of his pocket.*

Simeon All around the world people are dying right now – this very minute – from famine, disease, old age, natural disasters, murder. Their hour has come at the command of God, Fate, Universal Providence, bad luck. Aren't all those lives as precious as mine? Wouldn't one of them do? Why does it have to be me? Aren't there enough dead people in the world? Trouble is – I'm thinking too much about it – and the more I think. . . (*Inspects the coffin and arranges the wreaths around it tidily.*) Maybe if I just get used to the idea . . .

Climbs into the coffin. Pauses. Deep breath. Lies down.

Enter **Mary** *and* **Sadie**.

Mary They're coming!

Sadie They're coming!

Mary   Simeon?

Sadie   Where's he gone?

Mary *and* **Sadie** *run out again – different exit.*

Simeon *sits up, thinks, lies down again.*

Enter **Victor**, **Maggie**, **Al**, **Pugh**, **Rosie**, **MacLeod** *(with elements for Last Rites).*

Al   They brought him home a short while ago.

Victor   The crowd is gathering. Word has spread.

Al   People care. They really do.

Victor   We all care.

General mumbles of 'caring'.

Victor   I have composed a poem in his memory.

Pugh   My company is sponsoring a statue.

MacLeod   An application has already gone to the Vatican for his beatification.

Maggie   We're having a sponsored darts 'n' tarts night – raise money for the support fund, like.

Rosie   My group are holding a bare-breasted sit-in at the town hall.

Enter **Mary** *and* **Sadie**.

Mary   Al. Mr Bush – please help them to understand . . .

Al   It's all right, Mary.

Mary   No it's not. He didn't want to die.

Sadie   We're not blaming anybody.

Victor   But you must. Simeon did. He knew the cause of all his troubles.

Mary   Look at it from my point of view. I love him, and /

Al   Don't worry, Mrs Duff. I'll see that you never go without.

Maggie   Without what?

Victor   And after all he has been through – he is now at peace . . .

Mary *looks in the coffin for the first time and sees* **Simeon** – *faints.*

Sadie   What's the matter?

Sadie *sees* **Simeon** – *also faints.*

Victor   'For he being dead, with him is beauty slain / And, beauty dead, black chaos comes again . . .'

Pugh   I don't think he looks to bad, personally.

MacLeod   I've seen worse.

Sadie *and* **Mary** *come round.*

Sadie   Is he gone then?

Mary   Simeon. Sim! He's not, he's not . . . He can't be!

Pugh   In denial, see. I suppose it's to be expected.

Mary   He's alive, I tell you.

Sadie   He did take an awful bang to the head, Mary.

Al   That's one way of putting it.

Mary   But only a moment he was walking and talking and breathing and . . .

Victor   And now he is alive in a more powerful way than ever before.

MacLeod   He's dead.

Mary   No, no, no, no, no.

Sadie   He's sleeping . . .

MacLeod   The sleep of the righteous.

Mary   He's drunk.

Pugh   Deceased.

Sadie   Concussed!

Rosie   Conked out.

Mary   Alive, alive . . .

Victor   This is undignified. We must maintain an atmosphere of solemnity and reverence. Take them out, somebody.

Exit **Rosie** *and* **Maggie** *with* **Sadie** *and weeping* **Mary**.

MacLeod   How the poor woman is suffering with it.

Victor   We have to get her under control. It's a bit ugly at the moment. We need the widow looking more picturesque for the funeral.

Al   She'll come round. There's always a load of snot first up, but you soon dry out. Take me for instance. When I lost my darling wife I was in a shocking state. Poleaxed by grief, I was. Couldn't sleep for weeks after – and if you don't believe me, ask Maggie Johnson.

Pugh   He looks so peaceful – he could almost be alive.

MacLeod   The bloom hasn't yet faded from his cheeks. But his nose is dead all right. I'd better get on with it, I suppose. (*He starts to prepare to give* **Simeon** *the Last Rites.*)

Victor   Remember this moment, friends. History is made here. In the future, we will be able to say, 'I was in the room with the body of Simeon Duff' (*Strokes a tear away.*) I didn't cry when my own mother died, but . . .

Al   Perhaps now might be a good time to bring up the matter of payment.

Pugh   What for?

Al   For the corpse. Everything delivered according to our agreement. Cash on the nose – and, as the good Padre says, it's a dead nose!

Victor   Have you had the note copied and circulated?

Al   In the process as we speak.

Victor   Good. The worm will spread. The shot is fired – now let the world hear the report.

Pugh   You're expecting great things, Victor.

Victor   I would have preferred someone a little more important. Simeon Duff is hardly a loss to the world. Now, if he had been an eminent scientist, an artist, or a writer such Victor Stark . . . but in the end it doesn't matter who's in the coffin – what matters is how we serve him up to the nation as a martyr. It's my skill as a poet that will make or break this venture. I've started already. Quite by chance I met with that young student, Eddie Parker, just last night and I told him all about Simeon. I drew a picture of Duff that his own mother wouldn't recognise.

MacLeod   Please, gentlemen. I'm prepared now.

A bell.

Victor   Death, you see, is not infectious. But the cause of death is.

MacLeod   In the name of the Father, and of the Son, and of the Holy Ghost. Amen.

MacLeod *begins to perform the Last Rites.*

Enter **Choir** *to drown out* **MacLeod**'s *voice, singing* **Chesnokov Op. 40–2, The Pre-Eternal Council.**

Lights fade to black.

Act Five

The same.

Later that day.

Simeon *in the coffin.*

Beat.

Simeon *sits up.*

Voices off.

Simeon *lies back down.*

Enter **Chloe** *and* **George.**

Chloe   I heard they brought him here.

George   I don't think so, Ma'm'selle Chloe.

Chloe   Yes – look! He's here.

George   Already?

Chloe   Oh Simeon!

George   I mean, don't they have to pronounce death – certificates and so on. Formalities . . .

Chloe   Formalities. Ha! Now who's bourgeois? It was a crime passionnel. And I, for one, don't need a death certificate because I am the one who killed him.

George   I thought he shot himself.

Chloe   For me. Oh – how could I know when I spurned him that this would be the result? My mother was very beautiful, George. Her body drove men wild. As I myself blossomed into womanhood I too was desired by men, just the same. My eyes, my waist, my thighs, my breasts; dimples, freckles, goose pimples – it frightens me, George.

George *is desperately trying to listen to all this from a Marxist point of view.*

Chloe   When I was sixteen, I was trying on a pair of shoes in a shop and the assistant leant down and actually tried to suck my big toe! That kind of thing has been happening to me all my life – and now . . . this. Oh look at him George. Look on the face of a true lover.

George   I will look at him, Ma'm'selle Chloe. But I will look at him from a Marxist point of view. (**George** *looks into the coffin, swallows hard, and then back at* **Chloe**.) There.

Chloe   Look at him properly, George. Touch him. Kiss him.

George   I don't kiss.

Chloe   Take me to your room, George.

George   I can't do that, Ma'm'selle Chloe. You haven't been authorised.

Chloe   Comfort me. I cannot be alone with my body.

Chloe *thrusts herself onto* **George**, *who receives her awkwardly.*

Enter **Maggie**, **Al** *and* **Rosie** – *with* **Mary** *and* **Sadie**, *in mourning clothes.*

Victor *and* **Pugh** *following behind.*

Maggie   Do you mind. We're bringing in the grieving widow.

Al   Steady now, Mrs Duff.

Mary   Is he still there? Is he still dead?

Al   Don't crowd the widow now.

Sadie   It's true, Mary, God rest him. He must have had one of them explosions on the brain.

They file past the coffin and **Mary** *is seated.*

Victor (*to* **Pugh**)   It's a lovely spot in the graveyard. High up. Chose it myself.

Pugh   Location, location, location.

Victor   And all the invitations to the funeral have now gone out.

Al   I've done everyone I know.

Pugh   And me.

Victor   I just need to make sure Eddie Parker received his. It's imperative that he comes.

Al   Get one of the girls to chase him.

Victor   If he paid attention to them he wouldn't be any use to us. No – it has to come from me. I'll see him, don't worry. He is our gateway to the youth of England.

George (*to* **Victor**)   I didn't realise, this morning, when Simeon said he was going somewhere . . . I thought he was going to France.

Victor   Feeling a little squeamish, George. You'll have to toughen up, you know, come the Revolution.

George   I'll be ready.

Victor   Make sure you are, because 'something is rotten in the state of Denmark'.

George   Really? You mean it's started? At last! The false god of Capitalism is falling first in Denmark, who'd have thought it.

Victor   You idiot.

Mary   Oh Simeon. Why did you do it? Why?

Victor   He did it to rouse the people to political awareness.

George   I thought you said he did it for you.

Chloe   He did.

Mary   What?

Chloe   I'm sorry, Madame. He was obsessed.

Mary   Who the bloody hell are you? My Simeon loved me, and I loved him. He didn't die for you, you dirty scut. He didn't die for any of you. He didn't want to die at all.

Al   Now, Mary.

Mary   She's off her cake.

Victor   Simeon Duff was a martyr to many causes – overwhelmed by Truth. Unable to bear the burden of so much sorrow and injustice; incapable of finding an answer to the sufferings of the world in one creed, one dogma, one point of view. For him the struggle was too great and all his questions were ultimately transplanted by one overarching question – why live?

Mary   Oh Simeon.

Victor   And to that question, Simeon Duff had no answer but the answer we see before us now, laid in the coffin.

A bell sounds off stage.

Sadie   He's a beautiful speaker. I take it all back.

Enter **Father MacLeod** *– black soutane and cappello – Holy Water.*

MacLeod   We are ready to receive the body of this Christian martyr into the Church of the Immaculate Heart of Mary.

Al   I'm surprised, Father, that you're allowing a 'doubtful death' to be laid in consecrated ground.

MacLeod   Oh yes, we're not so inflexible as you might think. In the Church we have quite a lot of leeway.

Al   But aren't there certain rules . . .?

MacLeod   Ah, rules. Sometimes they're useful (*Splashing Holy Water round the coffin.*) and sometimes they're not. Let us pray.

George   I don't pray.

Exit **George**.

MacLeod   We have come to receive the body of our brother, Simeon. Simeon's death was a desperate plea for a return to a more spiritual way of life. He was a martyr for the one, true, Holy Catholic Church.

Victor (*mutters*)   Politics.

Pugh (*mutters*)   Business.

Chloe (*mutters*)   Love.

Rosie (*mutters*)   Sex.

Al   Please. We have all profited by this man's death – me more than anyone. And I just want to say something. (*Leans over the coffin.*) Simeon, I'm sorry. I'm genuinely sorry about all this. I know it's too late, but I'm asking you to forgive me. Forgive me, Simeon . . .

Simeon *sits up suddenly and embraces* **Al**.

Simeon   I forgive you, Al. Can you forgive me?

General screams and pandemonium.

Now, will someone get me something to eat. I'm STARVING!

Mary   Simeon! You are alive after all!

Simeon   Mary! Oh Mary, my darling. My beautiful wife, my love.

He leaps from the coffin and kisses **Mary** *passionately. She is frozen for a second and then starts hitting him violently.*

Mary   You selfish bastard. Do you know what I've been through today? First you were dead, then you weren't, then you were again, then . . . Oh God, Simeon I could kill you!

Simeon   Kill me, but not before I've had a sausage.

Mary   Oh, no. That's where all the trouble started.

Sadie   I made cheese pie.

Simeon   Mother, I love you.

Simeon *motions to embrace* **Sadie**, *who exits quickly to fetch pie.*

Simeon   Friends – if that's what I may call you. Friends, forgive me. I have laid here in this coffin all day, looking in on myself, listening to you – and do you know what I discovered? My appetite. I'm hungry. I want to eat. And when I've eaten, I want to live.

Victor   On what exactly? You have no job, no prospects . . .

Simeon   I have a stomach that feels the pangs of hunger. I have a heart that hammers in my chest and I don't want to die. Not for the nation, not for the economy, not for sex or God, or even for love.

A little squeak from **Chloe**.

Simeon   I'm sorry Chloe, but not even Eddie Parker is worth dying for.

Exits **Chloe**, *with a sob.*

Simeon   In the face of death nothing is dearer to a man than his own hand. (*Holds out his hand in wonder.*) Look at that! Look at it! Hands are amazing. Some people don't have any hands, you know, Victor? And I have two!

Victor   You miserable worm.

Simeon   No, not a worm, or a chicken, or a duck. A man. Just that.

Victor   One man is nothing compared with the greater common good.

Simeon *pulls the gun from the coffin and tosses it to* **Victor**.

Simeon   You do it then. Leave me out of it. I don't want to be turned into a shrine, or a slogan, or a soundbite. I don't need to be rich, or even successful. My very existence on this earth is enough to wonder at.

Pugh   You wanted to shoot yourself. You said you did.

Simeon   This morning I heard the dawn chorus outside my window. The birds don't think about posterity – they just do their thing and sing in the sun, shelter in the winter, and die when their wings and their hearts stop beating. Fame is nothing – especially when you have to be dead to achieve it. You said it Al, 'Life is beautiful' – only you didn't know what that meant. But I do. I do. The Universe is nearly fourteen billion years old – and every second of that time has plotted a course that led to the brief, beautiful existence of *me*. I don't think I'm the centre of the Universe – but I am a result of it – on the very outer edge, the vanguard of Time. Why would I sacrifice the few short precious years of consciousness that I've randomly been granted to breathe and eat and love, for the good opinion of people I'll never meet; for a symbolic place in a future that I'll know nothing of?

Enter **Sadie**, *with pie*.

Sadie   I'd put it to cool on the window-sill, but there's still a little warmth in it.

Simeon *sits and eats*.

Victor   There are people waiting to mourn you. An obituary is going in the paper . . .

Pugh   A bronze statue is being cast.

Maggie   Food is ordered for slap up wake at the Blind Piper.

Rosie (*realising*)   Hundreds of women are baring their breasts at the town hall.

Rosie *exits in panic*. **Al** *starts to follow*.

Maggie   Al . . . ? Al!

Exit **Al**, *followed by* **Maggie**.

Simeon   You can give them a coffin, can't you?

Victor   Without a corpse?

Simeon   Put a stack of political pamphlets in (*To* **Pugh**.) or your tax return (*To* **MacLeod**.) or a big gold crucifix – and nail the lid down. I won't tell.

Pugh   Can we have him arrested? It's fraud, isn't it?

MacLeod   Blasphemy.

Victor   It's treason. You treacherous bastard – I'll shoot you myself.

Victor *points gun at* **Simeon**.

Simeon (*rising to his feet*)   Right, right, right. OK! I've had enough of you. You haven't got the balls to kill yourselves, so why should I? I never did any harm. You say we should think about the 'common good' – but if I found out just one thing today, it's that we're all alone. So leave me be. I never hurt a soul my whole life through, and I'm not responsible for anyone but myself.

A bell tolls.

Choir (*off*)   Requiem aeternam . . .

MacLeod   Oh for God's sake! (*Calls off.*) Will you put a sock in it, he's not dead!

Choir (*off*)   Dona eis Domine.

Enter **Al**, *ashen, carrying a piece of paper.*

Choir (*off*)   Et lux perpetua luceat eis.

Al   It's Eddie.

Victor   Eddie Parker?

Al   He's committed suicide.

Simeon   Why? Why would he do that?

Al   He left a note.

Victor   What does it say?

Al *hands the paper to* **Victor**.

Al   He said, 'Simeon Duff is right.'

Victor (*reads*)   'Why live?'

Bell.

Three **Gypsy Women** *enter – as at the start of the play.*

Gypsies (*sing*)   **The Parting Glass (Traditional)**

>Of all the money that e'er I spent
>I've spent it in good company
>And all the harm that e'er I've done
>Alas it was to none but me
>And all I've done for want of wit
>To memory now I can't recall
>So fill to me the parting glass
>Good night and joy be with you all

All (*Sing.*)   Oh, all the comrades that e'er I had
>Are sorry for my going away
>And all the sweethearts that e'er I had
>Would wish me one more day to stay
>But since it falls unto my lot
>That I should rise and you should not
>I'll gently rise and I'll softly call
>Good night and joy be with you all
>Good night and joy be with you all

Simeon Duff

D McAndrew

C Nelson

O hear the ba-llad of Sim-e-on Duff. Life was hard and he'd had e-nough, mo-ney was tight as a ham-sters chuff_ for Sim-e-on, Sim-e-on Duff. The world was cruel to Sim-e-on Duff. Mad and mired in the deep-est slough. No-bo-dy seemed to give a stuff_ 'Bout Sim-e-on, Sim-e-on Duff. And when it seemed he had no choice this voice-less man, with debts piled high and bills un-paid, he ma-de a plan. No more pick-ing at na vel fluff. Prob-lem solved with a pinch of snuff, he said he'd do it, they called his bluff! O Sim-e-on, Sim-e-on Duff. O Sim-e-on, Sim-e-on, one in a mill-i-on Sim-e-on, Sim-e-on Duff.

Cardinal Puff

D McAndrew

C Nelson

craic. So - Drain the bo-ttle and drain the ba-rrel, yes drain it, ev - e - ry drop.

Once a Car-di- nal, al-ways a Card-i- nal!___   Drink and ne ver stop!

Printed in Great Britain
by Amazon